Fostering Resilient Learners

Praise for *Fostering Resilient Learners*

As a school counselor for the last 20 years, I am so grateful for this book! Kristin has served trauma-impacted children and families throughout her career and has incredibly effective ways of sharing all that she has learned. I am a stronger counselor and more effective leader in my building due to her influence. I am so excited that through this book, more people will be inspired to learn and grow in the important work of serving kids and families affected by trauma.

—Laurie Curran, elementary school counselor

The effects of chronic stress and adversity on children's learning, development, and behavior have been well documented in the literature over the past two decades. Kristin Souers not only is an expert and innovator in the field but also has a knack for translating the research into effective practice for children and adults alike. *Fostering Resilient Learners* is an excellent, practical resource for all adults working with and inside education systems, and I highly recommend it to better understand the needs of the whole child and to create the foundation for *all* students' learning and success.

—Natalie Turner, Assistant Director,
Child and Family Research Unit, Washington State University

As a client, I have benefited firsthand from the strategies Kristin teaches in creating a safe and secure learning environment. This book is worth every minute because these are relevant principles that work!

—E. W., parent

The information, strategies, and support that this book offers are what we need in our profession to truly leave no children behind. In implementing these strategies, you will shift your focus from reacting to negative student behavior to explaining and preventing negative student behavior. Once you can prevent getting "sucked into Oz," you can achieve all your goals for staff and students.

—Shannon Lawson, building principal

Fostering Resilient Learners

Strategies for Creating a
Trauma-Sensitive
Classroom

Kristin Souers with **Pete Hall**

ASCD | Alexandria, VA USA

1703 N. Beauregard St. • Alexandria, VA 22311-1714 USA
Phone: 800-933-2723 or 703-578-9600 • Fax: 703-575-5400
Website: www.ascd.org • E-mail: member@ascd.org
Author guidelines: www.ascd.org/write

Deborah S. Delisle, *Executive Director;* Stefani Roth, *Publisher;* Genny Ostertag, *Director, Content Acquisitions;* Julie Houtz, *Director, Book Editing & Production;* Miriam Goldstein, *Editor;* Donald Ely, *Senior Graphic Designer;* Mike Kalyan, *Manager, Production Services;* Valerie Younkin, *Production Designer;* Kyle Steichen, *Senior Production Specialist*

PAPERBACK ISBN: 978-1-4166-2107-2   ASCD product #116014   n1/16

PDF E-BOOK ISBN: 978-1-4166-2109-6; see Books in Print for other formats.

Quantity discounts: 10–49, 10%; 50+, 15%; 1,000+, special discounts (e-mail programteam@ascd.org or call 800-933-2723, ext. 5773, or 703-575-5773). For desk copies, go to www.ascd.org/deskcopy.

ASCD Member Book No. FY16-4A (Jan. 2016 PSI+). ASCD Member Books mail to Premium (P), Select (S), and Institutional Plus (I+) members on this schedule: Jan, PSI+; Feb, P; Apr, PSI+; May, P; Jul, PSI+; Aug, P; Sep, PSI+; Nov, PSI+; Dec, P. For current details on membership, see www.ascd.org/membership.

Library of Congress Cataloging-in-Publication Data
Names: Souers, Kristin, author. | Hall, Peter A., 1971- author.
Title: Fostering resilient learners : strategies for creating a trauma-sensitive classroom / Kristin Souers with Pete Hall.
Description: Alexandria, Virginia : ASCD, [2016] | Includes bibliographical references and index.
Identifiers: LCCN 2015037908 | ISBN 9781416621072 (pbk.)
Subjects: LCSH: Mentally ill children—Education. | Psychic trauma in children. | Post-traumatic stress disorder in children. | Educational   psychology.
Classification: LCC LC4181 .S68 2016 | DDC 371.94—dc23 LC record available at http://lccn.loc.gov/2015037908

23 22 21 20 19 18   6 7 8 9 10 11 12

To my children, Katlynn and Quade: you are the light of my life, and I learn from you every day. Thank you for being the amazing children you are. I am so blessed to be your mom! I love you both so very much!

—*Kristin Souers*

To Sienna, and to all the Siennas out there who need us to be at our very best every precious moment.

—*Pete Hall*

Fostering Resilient Learners

Strategies for Creating a
Trauma-Sensitive Classroom

Foreword

This is a book about opportunity and hope for addressing some of the wicked problems educators are asked to deal with every day. It reaffirms educators' current best practices while translating new science into sensible day-to-day educational practice. Grounded in years of lessons from the authors' experiences, this book offers a new way of thinking about student needs and the art of teaching.

I have had the privilege of being Kristin Souers's colleague for many years. Together, over the course of 10 years, we have developed and delivered a trauma-informed schools model. Kristin's commitment to the success of students, educators, and schools imbues our work, and she has enriched my own understanding of trauma and how to transform research into practice. Her passion for what works and for what is true shines throughout this book.

We now know that the piling on of adversity early in life is commonplace. Conservatively, one in three of us grow up with three or more powerful disruptive risks (adverse childhood experiences, or ACEs) to our development as human beings. The toxic stress that results from these ACEs can affect the pace and extent of brain development, the quality of our relationships, and our ability to manage ourselves. Taken together, these changes define what we mean by *trauma* and the potential for a lifetime of lost opportunities in education, work, relationships, and health.

Teachers were not taught how to identify and address the challenges resulting from trauma, but they face the impact of trauma in their classrooms every day. If it is not your child who has experienced trauma and struggles in school, it is the child sitting next to your child. Not every student has a significant trauma history, but the needs of those who do can define the success of the entire classroom.

Our limitations in recognizing and responding appropriately to trauma are a huge factor in school systems' failure to produce the results they want. For students, trauma interferes with being present with a "learning-ready" brain, contributes to chronic attendance problems, and is a major driver for the behavior problems that exhaust educators and demotivate classmates. For educators, unaddressed student trauma is a major contributor to frustration, low job satisfaction, and burnout.

The good news is that we now know a great deal about how to help children and adults recover from trauma. Risk is not destiny. We know that the brain, particularly in childhood, has an extraordinary ability to adapt and recover. The biggest factor in making these critical repairs to the brain? Relationship. In fact, high-quality relationships are essential not only to children's development but also to our own growth.

In this era of high-stakes testing and accountability, we must start a national conversation about moving relationship to the center of educational practice. This focus on relationship doesn't diminish the role of high-quality curricula and strong pedagogy, but it does mean that your strategies won't succeed if you can't connect meaningfully with students.

As this book goes to press, "trauma-informed" is a big buzzword in education. The challenge is how to translate this relatively recent interest into enduring shifts in policy and practice. Current discussion about trauma is part of a historic period of change in how we think about ourselves and our communities and helping people. Educators can be a great part of the solution and champion the larger conversation we need to have with parents and our communities.

As an educator, you don't have a choice about being in the trauma business. You *do* have a choice in what you do about it. This book is a practical tool to help you begin to incorporate trauma understanding and management skills into your daily practice. It is a guide to understanding trauma, building the strong relationships needed to reach the academic outcomes you want, perceiving what students need to break the cycle, and scaffolding new learning for all struggling learners. Simply put, this book offers a path to sustainable change.

Despite the sobering evidence of the profound effect trauma has on our schools, this book is about hope and growth. Rather than providing a prescriptive curriculum or a complicated framework, this book will help you use good science to adapt to the needs of students who have experienced and continue to be exposed to trauma. It will show you how your practice is the vehicle for change. Thank you for being part of the conversation.

Christopher Blodgett, Ph.D.
Washington State University
Summer 2015

Acknowledgments

This is my favorite section of this book to write because it gives me the opportunity to express my eternal gratitude to all who have given me the knowledge and the means to write this book.

First and foremost, I must thank Pete (along with his terrific family, who gave us time to work together). If it weren't for him, this book wouldn't exist, and I wouldn't have had the opportunity to work with Genny and Miriam at ASCD, both of whom were amazing. Thanks, Pete, for believing in me and for being my teammate. I will forever remember the lunch at Subway that launched this whole process. You have been truly inspirational and motivational. You are a maverick, and I am with you 100 percent!

To my amazing mentors and colleagues: I have been blessed to work with extraordinary people who get people, and I thank you. I'd like to give a special shout-out to Chris Blodgett (boss man, thanks for your unwavering belief in my ability to do this work justice); Roy Harrington (you are so great at helping me to stay at 10,000 feet—thanks for challenging me and keeping me focused on what matters); Natalie Turner (my like-minded work partner in crime); Dennis McGaughy (thanks for letting me take risks in this field and advocate for folks in a different way); Kent Hoffman (the man who taught me the meaning of attachment); Deanda Roberts (my sounding board and constant regulator—I don't know where I would be without you); and, finally, the many other outstanding researchers and fellow passionate advocates for this work. Without you, none of this would have happened.

To the wonderful clients, students, education professionals, and caregiving professionals who were willing to trust me and be vulnerable with me: thank you for your awe-inspiring strength, resilience, and honesty, and for enlightening others with your experiences. You all inspire me daily, and you gave me the courage to put my passion onto paper. I hope I did you justice.

To Pat Souers: although our lives may have turned out differently than we had hoped, you have offered constant and consistent support. Your belief in my ability to do this work has never wavered, and I am grateful.

To my dearest friend, Laurie Curran: words cannot express how grateful I am for you and our friendship! Thank you for your long hours of listening and processing and advising. You keep me steady and true. I am grateful for your unwavering faith in me and my ability to do this work.

Finally, thanks go to my family and friends for their continual support and encouragement. Mom, Dad, Steph, Mark, Drew, Jack, Ian, and Luke: thanks for being who you are and for doing all that you do! I am blessed to call you my family. To all my friends who stood by me through this process: your support and encouragement helped immensely, and I am so lucky to have you in my life. A special shout-out goes to Fr. Paul Fitterer, Andrea McFarland, Bonnie Wagner, and Yvonne and Jeff Trudeau, who always asked how it was going and were staunch supporters of the project.

—Kristin Souers

We owe a tremendous debt of gratitude to the good folks at ASCD, who acted on their vision to include this perspective as part of the critical conversations within the Whole Child Initiative. We cannot ignore childhood trauma and its effects, and ASCD has stepped forward with a strong voice. Special thanks are reserved for our wise and meticulous editor, Miriam Goldstein, who checked and double-checked to make sure each word conveyed precisely what we intended, and for the incomparable Genny Ostertag, whose insightful questioning and relentless energy helped shape this work.

—Pete Hall

Introduction

Raise levels of academic achievement for every student.

That's our mission in schools. Education is the gatekeeper to choices in life, and it is how we gauge our youth's readiness for a productive entry into society. Teaching students the three *R*s is, of course, a massive responsibility and a great first step in preparing them for graduation and beyond. Yet it's not enough. There are additional *R*s that our students must learn: Responsibility. Respect. Resilience. Relationship.

It seems as though more and more students are arriving at school lacking these and other crucial skills. Instead, they step into our schools toting heavy burdens: the stress of overwhelming trauma and the scars of neglect and abuse. The experience of trauma has dramatically altered the landscape of the schools we work in.

I have a singular focus: to help you equip your students with the skills to succeed. I want to support you in creating a safe and predictable space that fosters not only students' learning but also their overall development. My professional role is a licensed mental health therapist, and I have partnered with veteran school principal and current education consultant Pete Hall to write this important book. Although our two roles are different, the approaches we take are often similar. You, the reader, have the most important role of all: directly influencing the environment in which students face daily academic and interpersonal challenges. Teachers, parents, guardians, mental health professionals, counselors, caretakers, administrators, support personnel, and anyone else who has a hand (and a heart) in the education of our youth: this book is for you.

What's in This Book

In Chapters 1 and 2, I discuss what trauma is and what forms it may take. Research on trauma has exploded over the last 10 years, and we now know more than ever the significance of its effect on development and learning. In these early chapters, I introduce you to the biological nature of trauma and connect it to the purpose of the strategies I share throughout this book. I discuss the prevalence of **adverse childhood experiences** (ACEs) and explain how these **not-OK events**—a euphemism for trauma and other damaging occurrences—affect students' readiness to learn. You will learn that while each child's narrative is important, the simple fact that a student has experienced trauma is all educators really need to know. Because the statistics are so overwhelming, I encourage you to view every student as though he or she has experienced trauma or is exposed to chronic stress.

In subsequent chapters, I ask you to shift your focus. I instill hope. Current statistics suggest that 70 percent of trauma-affected youth go on to lead successful, productive lives. Our goal is 100 percent—and you can help make it happen. By adopting a strength-based approach, you will see the wonder beneath the chaos. By seeking solutions rather than dwelling on problems, you will discover the path to success in partnership with each student. By understanding a piece of the "why" behind behaviors, you will foster a safe and secure environment in which "it's OK to be not-OK." And by both nurturing and holding high expectations for your students, you will build relationships that enable students to grow, thrive, and learn at high levels.

Chapters 3 through 15 are full of practical strategies for creating what I call a **trauma-sensitive learning environment**: a classroom, school, nook, or any other teaching location in which each and every student is healthy, safe, engaged, supported, and challenged (the five tenets of ASCD's whole child approach). The strategies are organized around four primary themes: *self-awareness, relationship, belief,* and *live, laugh, love.* You'll notice that my discussion of the strategies goes back and forth between teachers and students. This is intentional, because every bit of advice applies to educators and learners alike.

I have used each of the strategies extensively in my practice during the last two decades. According to the needs of my clients, I select the strategies that best support their healing, growth, and pursuit of peace. In this book, I share the strategies that tend to yield the greatest benefit. These are the proven, reliable approaches—the ones I have taught counselors, educators, caregivers, and other professionals across the United States. I share them because they work.

Although the strategies themselves are helpful, it is important to keep in mind that their larger purpose is to shift our focus to the positive. They are a reminder that we should recalibrate how we view student misbehaviors. They are a reminder that as the adults, we should, to use a quote from the Circle of Security project (Marvin, Cooper, Hoffman, & Powell, 2002), be "bigger, stronger, wiser, and kind." If we aren't willing to open our minds and hearts to this new belief system, the strategies in this book will be neat and useful, but they will not be sufficient.

 Pete and I have created an online guide to encourage reflection and extension of the ideas in this book. We use the icon pictured to the left throughout the book to indicate the availability of online forms to fill in or print out. You can download this guide at www.ascd.org/ASCD/pdf/books/souers2016.pdf. Use the password "souers116014" to unlock the PDF.

Why Did I Write This Book?

During my 20-year career as a licensed mental health professional, I have had the pleasure of meeting and learning from some of the most acclaimed researchers in the field of trauma. Thanks to their skills, knowledge, and perseverance in raising awareness of this prevalent issue, we collectively have much more information to help us understand trauma and its impact on learning and development.

After much urging from my colleagues, clients, and the teachers, counselors, and administrators with whom I work in schools, I decided to share my learning with you. There are two major reasons for this book. First, it is important to me to help others experience good health and abundant happiness—and if there's a chance I can do that, I am going to try. Second, Pete has been very persistent at holding me to my word and quoting Carl Jung at me ("You are what you do, not what you say you'll do"). As a collaborator and partner, Pete supports and augments the findings and practices I share in this book with timely insights from the school perspective. I have woven his "Pete's Practice" sections into every chapter to bring the strategies to life. The following is the first in this series.

PETE'S PRACTICE

As a longtime educator and a former elementary and middle school principal, I have seen firsthand the challenges that trauma drops on our students. In classrooms across the United States, students struggle with their demons and try to make sense of the world, while the world demands greater academic performance regardless of their circumstances.

During the last 14 years, I have served as an assistant principal or a principal in four public schools in Reno, Nevada, and Spokane, Washington. In those schools and in the schools I've visited across the country as a consultant, the effects of trauma know no boundaries. Students struggle with not-OK situations at all socioeconomic levels, in all cultures, at all grade levels and ages, and in all settings.

It was in Spokane that I first had the opportunity to hear Kristin speak at a workshop for educators. The information was so heart-wrenching, so real, and so daunting that it immediately struck a chord with me. Kristin's take on the epidemic of trauma was succinct and incredibly potent: we can't do anything about the trauma our kids experience, but we can do a lot to provide a trauma-sensitive learning environment for all students. Immediately, I recruited Kristin to work with my teachers, and the impact of her work has been staggering.

Often, teachers and school administrators fight the battle of accountability versus availability, alternating between pushing students with rigorous expectations and nurturing students with sensitivity and care. We needn't choose one or the other. It is high time that we embrace both. Every classroom can and should be a safe place for students to live, learn, develop, and meet high academic standards. Together, we can accomplish anything we set our minds and hearts to.

I was thrilled that Kristin asked me to lend a practitioner's perspective to this project. She has poured her heart and soul into supporting the teachers and professionals who work with our most vulnerable young people, and her strategies work. While I share an anecdote here and there to show the strategies working in the field, I am forever inspired by her wisdom as I strive to positively influence every student I encounter. Read, learn, and find the courage to embrace a mindset for establishing a trauma-sensitive learning environment in every district, school, and classroom.

A Note on Testimonials

Sprinkled throughout this book are some testimonials to the power of trauma-sensitive practices from clients and education professionals whom I've worked with over the years. My hope is that they offer an additional perspective to help you make sense of this material. Because of counselor-patient privilege and the importance of confidentiality, many of these quotations must remain anonymous, but I believe they're important to share. Here is the first, from a 6th grade teacher:

> Over my 25 years as an educator in a low-income, highly diverse school setting, I have worked hard to meet the needs of all the kids who come to my school. After working with Kristin Souers over the last few years, I have gained insight into the effects of trauma on the brain, and I have learned and incorporated strategies that have allowed me to be a more effective educator for all kids.
>
> The most immediate example is a student named "Joe," who spent every day in a self-contained behavior intervention room. His behavior problems stemmed from the abuse and neglect he suffered early in childhood. Joe once recounted a time when his father got so angry after Joe took his place on the couch that he picked him up and threw him across the room into a table. Joe was 5.
>
> Needless to say, Joe would act out angrily toward any frustration encountered in the classroom. But thanks to Kristin's lessons on the brain, lid-flip [a term used for when students "flip their lids" or have a meltdown], and grace, I gained insight into Joe's triggers. As a result, I have been able to successfully work and communicate with Joe to the point that he has had zero episodes of lid flipping and absolutely no office or disciplinary referrals in the two and a half months since he moved to my classroom. We have used Kristin's regulation strategies to help him monitor where he's at and succeed in the regular education classroom.

You Can Make a Difference

Reading this book does not guarantee that you will become the new "trauma guru," nor does it mean that you will immediately become trauma-sensitive in your practice with students. That part is up to you. True change does not come from reading a book or attending a class; it occurs when you make a commitment to change, when you empower your colleagues to see this as a real issue and collectively alter your approaches to incorporate a trauma-sensitive lens. We have a responsibility to educate every single child who enters our schoolhouses. Throughout your reading and your professional work, I urge you to do more, to be thoughtful, and to cultivate a trauma-sensitive learning environment for all students across all settings. An elementary-level educator shares the effect such changes have had on her practice, her school, and her students:

> In deepening my understanding of trauma and its effects on children, I have learned to look for triggers and root causes of a student's actions. I have learned to look at a student's ability to cope with present circumstances and react accordingly, providing the support and tools needed to give the child a sense of security and control. When students are taught coping skills and productive ways to communicate their needs, their behavior, social skills, and sense of self-worth improve. I have seen how positive praise can completely change a child's behavior. When a school staff receives trauma training and implements trauma-sensitive practices, students thrive.

I have spent my entire working life with people who have experienced adversity. It is amazing to me how many people encounter severe hardship in their lifetimes. You yourself have likely experienced some form of adversity. I hope that this book both empowers you in your learning and instills hope in your practice.

PART I
Trauma

Children are like wet cement. Whatever falls on them makes an impression.

—Haim Ginnot

. . . .

Pete and I talk a great deal about how we're in the middle of a "perfect storm" for education. Public accountability for educators is at an all-time high. Teachers are absorbing the blows of new evaluation systems, the advent of Common Core State Standards, debates over merit pay, rampant loss of tenure and job security, widespread fear of school shootings and security issues, the growing ranks of families in poverty, and a host of other challenges. That list doesn't even include our mandate to educate every child who walks through our doors, including the hungry, the angry, the anxious, the lonely, the tired, and the trauma-affected.

No one disagrees that students should be held to the highest standard of learning. Where conflict tends to occur is in how we tackle that goal. For many young people who have experienced trauma, success—academic or otherwise—seems out of reach. How do we support students who arrive at school affected by trauma and other not-OK experiences? How do we provide environments that are safe and predictable *and* motivational for learning?

Before we answer these questions, it is important to acknowledge some fundamental truths:

1. Trauma is real.

2. Trauma is prevalent. In fact, it is likely much more common than we care to admit.

3. Trauma is toxic to the brain and can affect development and learning in a multitude of ways.

4. In our schools, we need to be prepared to support students who have experienced trauma, even if we don't know exactly who they are.

5. Children are resilient, and within positive learning environments they can grow, learn, and succeed.

Those of us working in the caregiving field have long seen the effects that trauma has on young people. We have said, "I think this is a really big deal," and we were right. Thanks to the pioneering research of Vincent Felitti and Robert Anda and their colleagues (Felitti et al., 1998), who launched a landmark study investigating how ACEs contribute negatively to overall health, this globally significant issue can no longer be ignored. This study and those that followed opened our eyes to the fact that trauma is bigger than just a mental health issue— it's *everyone's* issue. After all, the adults providing services to youth are affected by their students' trauma; what's more, they are equally likely to have experienced trauma themselves.

It follows, then, that the issue of trauma pertains to you, the reader, as well as to your most vulnerable students. Now I'll ask you to be reflective: why did you choose this profession? What motivated you to enter the field, and what keeps you here? My colleagues and I ask these questions often in our trainings and consulting work. It is a powerful and foundational way to start connecting to those we work with. Many educators I've worked with reply that they believe they were "born to do this," that they understand what children need, and that they want to be able to address those needs in a helpful way. Some do it because they experienced trauma themselves and can empathize or connect with children who may also be experiencing adversity, while others had a positive experience with an educational professional and want to provide the same for the next generation. Others enter the field because their own experiences in education were not positive, and they want to provide students with a better experience than their own. Some are still searching for the answers to these questions. Take a moment and think of your own answers: why are you here, and why do you stay?

1

Understanding Trauma and the Prevalence of the Not-OK

It is an ultimate irony that at the time when the human is most vulnerable to the effects of trauma—during infancy and childhood—adults generally presume the most resilience. (Perry, Pollard, Blakley, Baker, & Vigilante, 1995)

· · · · · · · · · · · · · · · ·

From the Outside In... and the Inside Out

As a mental health therapist with more than two decades of experience working with children and families, I have seen firsthand the struggles that affect people's happiness, relationships, and coping ability. Not surprisingly, these struggles bleed into the school environment.

Collaborating closely with education professionals, principals, teachers, and counselors, I know that students' complicated, stressful lives can create conditions that present massive obstacles to learning.

Educators have long known that what happens outside school can have a profound effect on what happens in school. When the Equality of Educational Opportunity Study was published in 1966, lead researcher James Coleman concluded that the home environment was more predictive of student success than was schooling (Coleman et al., 1966). The "Coleman Study" was an important piece of the educational sociology puzzle and opened the door for further investigation into the external factors that influence academic achievement.

Early research into this phenomenon included explorations of the racially biased orientation of the school institution, student IQ, parental attitudes about school, socioeconomic status, parents' educational attainment, access to resources, vocabulary development, primary language, structures for completing homework and studying, diet and exercise, and student motivation, among other factors. A full library's worth of research explained why some students were successful in school and others weren't (see Hattie, 2009, for a meta-analysis of external factors affecting student achievement).

As an educator, you don't need a peer-edited research article to validate what your gut and your experience have already told you is true: a student's life outside school matters.

What Is Trauma?

Let's explore the idea of trauma in a little more depth. The word itself has gained a great deal of attention in recent years, although not without a significant amount of misunderstanding. In 1980, when post-traumatic stress disorder (PTSD) was first included in the *Diagnostic and Statistical Manual of Mental Disorders* (*DSM-III*), the diagnosis focused on a list of narrowly defined catastrophic events (e.g., war, torture, rape, natural disasters, plane crashes) rather than what may be defined as ordinary stressors (e.g., divorce, poverty, serious illness). Recent revisions of the manual (*DSM-5* was published in 2013), however, acknowledge the wide range of environmental, interpersonal, and experiential events that result in similar trauma-induced symptoms (Friedman, 2013). As the term *trauma* has become more mainstream, its definition has become broader and varies across fields. For the purposes of this book, I go by the following definition:

> Trauma is an exceptional experience in which powerful and dangerous events overwhelm a person's capacity to cope. (Rice & Groves, 2005, p. 3)

The term *complex trauma* was first explored in 2003 by the National Child Traumatic Stress Network's Complex Trauma Task Force, a collective of professionals representing a dozen universities, hospitals, trauma centers, and health programs across the United States. This term emerged from the recognition that many people experience multiple adversities over the course of their lifetime. The task force's concise and useful definition of *complex trauma* appears in the white paper *Complex Trauma in Children and Adolescents*:

> Complex trauma exposure refers to the simultaneous or sequential occurrences of child maltreatment—including emotional abuse and neglect, sexual abuse, physical abuse, and witnessing domestic violence—that are chronic and begin in early childhood.… Complex trauma outcomes refer to the range of clinical symptomatology that appears after such exposures. (Cook, Blaustein, Spinazzola, & van der Kolk, 2003, p. 5)

Note that these definitions focus on the *impact* of the events, not the *nature* of the events. Although some events (the death of a parent or surviving the September 11, 2001, terrorist attacks on the World Trade Center, for example) may warrant a label of trauma in their own right, we all respond differently to trauma. Our own experiences and interpretations influence the degree of impact we feel following exposure to a traumatic event.

More Than Their Story

When schools first started integrating trauma awareness about 10 years ago, they tended to emphasize the events themselves and the details of those experiences. Educators and other professionals felt compelled to learn a student's "story" as a means of understanding his or her behavior. That approach often led to getting caught up in the trauma narrative rather than supporting and understanding the effect of that event on the young person. It's not that a person's story isn't important, but educators don't always have the luxury of knowing the story. We do, however, see the story's lingering effects.

For instance, let's say I work with two children who have had similar traumatic experiences: they both have a parent who has been incarcerated for the last two years, and they rarely get to see that parent. Although that life event is devastating for us to consider, the two young people have dramatically different responses: one is unable to process the reality and shuts down whenever something evokes a memory of his parent, while the other functions relatively well, compensating by building a stronger bond with the remaining parent. It is much more helpful for me to monitor the *effect* of the event on each individual, not to preoccupy myself with the details of the event itself.

This shift in perspective prompts us to be more sensitive to that effect and thus better foster healing and growth. Moreover, by altering our approach, we can begin to see students as more than their story. All too often, we reduce students to their experiences and make decisions about their capabilities based on those experiences. Changing our focus enables us to concentrate on nurturing the whole child and creating trauma-sensitive learning environments for all students.

ACEs Wild

In the late 1990s, Dr. Robert Anda and Dr. Vincent Felitti led a collaborative project between the Centers for Disease Control and the Department of Preventive Medicine at Kaiser Permanente in San Diego, California, to explore the relationship between children's emotional experiences and their subsequent mental and physical health as adults. This groundbreaking research (Felitti et al., 1998) revealed a strong correlation between adverse childhood experiences and adult health and, perhaps more significantly, signaled that these ACEs were far more prevalent than previously thought.

What constitutes an ACE? Many of us can probably come up with some ideas, but the initial eight ACEs that Felitti and colleagues studied were

- Substance abuse in the home.
- Parental separation or divorce.
- Mental illness in the home.
- Witnessing domestic violence.
- Suicidal household member.
- Death of a parent or another loved one.
- Parental incarceration.
- Experience of abuse (psychological, physical, or sexual) or neglect (emotional or physical).

Many would argue now, and I would agree, that the list is not complete and should include other experiences, such as exposure to a natural disaster, criminal behavior in the home, terminal or chronic illness of a family member, military deployment of a family member, war exposure, homelessness, and victimization or bullying.

Despite this limitation, the details of the original ACE Study are fascinating. Anda and Felitti collected data from more than 17,000 adult patients who were insured by the major insurance provider in Southern California (Kaiser Permanente), tallying how many ACEs from the list each respondent had experienced. Each ACE listed was given a value of 1, so individuals reporting none of the above would have an ACE score of 0, whereas those who experienced all of the ACEs would have a score of 8. The researchers found that more than half of their subjects had experienced at least one ACE during their youth. Roughly 25 percent had experienced multiple ACEs, and 1 in 16 had an ACE score of 4 or above (Felitti et al., 1998). Not only did this study's result shock the belief systems of many people working in the caregiving fields, but it also helped dispel the myth that trauma happens only in populations of poverty. Although living in poverty increases the likelihood of ACE exposure, poverty itself is not considered an adverse childhood experience. This study supported what many of us already knew: trauma does not discriminate. It happens everywhere—across all races, religions, socioeconomic levels, and family systems.

One of the more profound implications of this study was the acknowledgment of the prevalence of trauma in our society. One might even hypothesize that these numbers were low estimates of the actual occurrences, owing to social taboos against seeking or sharing this type of information and the fact that the traumatic experiences were self-reported. In fact, in two similar studies (Breslau, Kessler, & Chilcoat, 1998; Burns, 2005), more than 90 percent of respondents reported at least one lifetime traumatic event. These studies have been replicated with hundreds of thousands of subjects and across several arenas (including, for example, health care, education, and military), but the results remain consistent. These findings have been so powerful that many states are incorporating ACE awareness into their state studies and census data.

Effect of ACEs on Adult Health

The original ACE Study investigated the relationship between ACEs and overall health and found, quite simply, that the higher an individual's ACE score was, the more likely it was that he or she would adopt or present with significant health-concerning outcomes, such as chronic obstructive pulmonary disease, hepatitis, sexually transmitted disease, intravenous drug use, depression, obesity, attempted suicide, or early death. In fact, there is a clear "dose effect," meaning the likelihood of having physical or mental health issues later in life increases in direct correlation to an individual's ACE score (Felitti et al., 1998).

Those working in the medical and mental health fields have long known that trauma exposure is toxic to the human body, and the ACE Study gave health professionals permission to begin to significantly address this issue on a global level.

Effect of ACEs on Children

The ACE Study shows a remarkable link between not-OK childhood events and health issues later in life. What the original ACE research did not explore, however, was the immediate effect that these trau matic experiences had on children. This is crucial information that can inform educators' practice and the supports we offer to the young people under our care.

First, is childhood trauma as prevalent as the original ACE Study suggested? Sadly, yes. Recent research indicates that there are now more children affected by trauma than ever before:

• Nearly 35 million U.S. children have experienced at least one type of childhood trauma (National Survey of Children's Health, 2011/2012).

• One study (Egger & Angold, 2006) of young children ages 2–5 found that 52 percent had experienced a severe stressor in their lifetime.

• A report of child abuse is made every 10 seconds (ChildHelp, 2013).

• In 2010, suicide was the second leading cause of death among children ages 12–17 (Centers for Disease Control and Prevention, 2011).

Having established the continued prevalence of trauma, let's look at how these experiences affect children's educational outcomes. Inspired by the original ACE Study, Dr. Chris Blodgett and his research team (Blodgett, 2012) at Washington State University's Area Health Education Center conducted its own adverse childhood experiences study in 2011, investigating the effect of the same eight ACEs on the educational outcomes of elementary school students (ages 5–11) in Spokane County, Washington. The results confirmed the pervasiveness of ACEs:

- Forty-five percent of students had at least one ACE.
- Twenty-two percent of students had multiple ACEs.
- One in 16 students had an ACE score of 4 or higher.

Simultaneously, it emerged that ACEs have a powerful negative effect on students' readiness to learn, leading to the "triple whammy" of school troubles in attendance, behavior, and coursework (the ABCs). Students showed progressively higher incidents of scholastic struggles as their ACE scores rose, again revealing the "dose effect" suggesting that the number of traumatic occurrences matters even more than their severity. For example, a student with one adverse childhood experience was 2.2 times more likely than was a student with no ACEs to have serious attendance issues, a student with two ACEs was 2.6 times more likely to have these issues, and a student with three or more ACEs was 4.9 times more likely to have these issues. Figure 1.1 summarizes Blodgett's team's findings.

Note that there is a fourth column labeled "Health." Blodgett and his team found a direct link between childhood trauma and physical health, documenting higher rates of frequent illness, obesity, asthma, and speech problems in students with higher ACE scores. These results further support the original ACE Study's findings that ACEs are toxic to the body.

FIGURE 1.1
Correlation Between Number of ACEs and Struggles with School and Health

	Attendance	Behavior	Coursework	Health
3+ ACEs	4.9	6.1	2.9	3.9
2 ACEs	2.6	4.3	2.5	2.4
1 ACE	2.2	2.4	1.5	2.3
No known ACEs	1.0	1.0	1.0	1.0

The more ACEs a student experienced, the more likely he or she was to experience serious school and health issues.

How Trauma Affects the Brain

So how, exactly, does exposure to trauma affect educational outcomes? Simply put, trauma is toxic to the brain as well as to the body. There has been vast research conducted on the brain in the last two decades that challenges much of how we have historically interpreted the brain and its function. Scientists have discovered a new way of looking at the power of nurture in human development. Further, the increasing awareness of the effects of trauma on the brain has offered tremendous insight into the role trauma exposure plays in development, especially in childhood.

In the midst of extreme stress, our bodies are forced to respond via a heightened state of alert known as the *flight, fight, or freeze response*. Our bodies were designed to be in that state only for brief periods, and only in the face of extreme danger. But when children are exposed to complex or acute trauma, the brain shifts its operation from development to stress response, which can have lasting repercussions. According to Harvard University professor Jack Shonkoff (2009),

In contrast to normal or tolerable stress, which can build resilience and properly calibrate a child's stress-response system, toxic stress is caused by extreme, prolonged adversity in the absence of a supportive network of adults to help the child adapt. When it occurs, toxic stress can actually damage the architecture of the developing brain, leading to disrupted circuits and a weakened foundation for future learning and health. (para. 4)

When brains are triggered by threat or perception of threat, they release chemicals into the body to allow us to "survive" those states of stress. When released in large doses, these chemicals become toxic to the body and can create significant impairment in development. Because the fetal, infant, and early childhood brain is so sensitive, chronically elevated levels of stress hormones can significantly disrupt the development of the brain in a multitude of ways, affecting learning, memory, mood, relational skills, and aspects of executive functioning (Shonkoff & Garner, 2012)—all required for success in a classroom setting. In Chapter 2, I further explore the educational implications of these negative effects.

PETE'S PRACTICE

Having served as a school administrator in extremely challenging schools for nearly a decade before meeting Kristin, I was sure I had seen it all. However, when she shared the statistics on childhood trauma and the effect that exposure can have on students' development and achievement, I was floored. It's an epidemic! How could this not have been part of my training? How could this huge aspect of our society and our profession remain relatively hidden and unaddressed?

Immediately, I began to work more closely with my administrative team, counselors, secretaries, and teachers to learn as much as possible about our students. What we uncovered—that more than 100 of the 500 students in my elementary school had (currently or recently) at least one parent incarcerated—was just the tip of the iceberg. We vowed to continue our investigation and to learn more about how we could provide a trauma-sensitive learning environment for all our students. It was an urgent wake-up call for all of us.

Wrapping It Up

Exposure to multiple and severe stressors can profoundly affect how children interpret their world. The more ACEs a child is exposed to, the greater the likelihood that he or she will experience developmental delays and health problems down the line. Increasing our awareness of ACEs in children and looking at our students through a trauma-sensitive lens open up an opportunity for us to approach teaching and learning in new ways.

Further, when we start to look at the prevalence of the adversity that many of us have faced in our own lives, we must also celebrate the power of resilience. Many of us have found a way to survive the not-OK. As professionals, how can we foster that same resilience in students that we were able to muster up to survive our own experiences?

We know that childhood trauma has become an epidemic. No one is immune: trauma occurs everywhere, in all populations and circumstances, at every socioeconomic level, across ethnic and cultural lines, within all religions, and at all levels of education (ChildHelp, 2013). Because trauma's effect often presents itself as a mental health issue, the need for services is growing substantially. Yet research reveals that only a minority of children receive services: according to the Surgeon General's Report, "about 75 to 80 percent of children with a serious emotional disturbance fail to receive specialty services, and, according to family members, the majority of these children fail to receive any services at all." According to Kutash, Duchnowski, and Lynn (2006), the vast majority of children receive no mental health services, and among those who do, most receive the services at school.

Children with mental health issues are not required to obtain professional mental health services, but they are legally obligated to attend school. Thus, school is the one place where we are guaranteed access to our trauma-affected children. Our students need us to create a trauma-sensitive learning environment for them.

This is why you're reading this book.

Reflective Questions

1.   Exploration of trauma sometimes launches a "nature versus nurture" debate. Why do you suppose some children are more strongly affected by certain events than others are? What does this suggest for us as professionals?

2.   What are your initial responses to the prevalence of trauma? Are you surprised? Why or why not?

3.   Review the original ACE Study's list of stressors. What might you add to that list? What do you see significantly affecting our students today?

4.   Kristin and Pete both refer to trauma as an epidemic. How much "airtime" has the topic received in your trainings, either preservice or in the field?

5.   Take a look at your class list or case roster. Based on facts that you know, how many of your students have an ACE score of 1? Two? Three or higher?

6.   Given the information above, how might you shift your approach in working with these vulnerable children?

7. What steps can you take to bring this important topic into your professional conversations? How might that provide an avenue to better support our students?

2

The Manifestation of ACEs in the Classroom

Kids do well if they can.

—Ross Greene, *Lost at School*

. . . .

Now that we know how prevalent trauma is, let's discuss its effect on the education profession: why is it relevant to us? What do the data on ACEs really mean for us? What are the implications for the work we do with students and their families? How do ACEs affect learning? With all the pressure we're under to push students toward mastery of grade-level standards, where does the trauma awareness piece fit in, and how can we incorporate it in a way that eases our burdens instead of adding to them?

Quite plainly, I believe that if our students aren't in the *learning mode*—a term coined by Pete's mentor, Frank C. Garrity, that refers to mental, physical, emotional, spiritual, and psychological readiness to learn—they simply will not learn. And students suffering from the effects of trauma are definitely *not* in the learning mode. If we want to meet our mission of ensuring high levels of learning for every student, we must first ensure that students are in a safe place.

Survival Mode

When humans sense that we are in danger, our brains switch to *survival mode*, triggering a flight, fight, or freeze response within us. In this mode, our body's sole mission is to escape danger and return as quickly as possible to a regulated and safe state. Universally, according to our biological makeup, we choose *flight* first. We have been hard-wired to avoid and escape from dangerous situations. When we cannot escape, our backup plan is to *fight*. Then there are the times when we cannot connect with our biological training or process our current reality effectively, which leaves us in a state of limbo. Unable to think clearly or determine a course of action, we *freeze*.

Here's a scenario to illustrate the flight, fight, or freeze response in action. Imagine you are in a room on the eighth story of a building participating in a workshop. The room is full of adults whose ages range from early 20s to late 60s. There is a pregnant woman in the room, and a man on crutches. As you listen to the two presenters, the ceiling suddenly shakes, and picture frames fall off the walls. Clearly, there is a threat, and everyone in the room immediately enters survival mode. First, everyone goes into flight mode: they know they need to escape the dangerous situation and find safety. However, some in the room do not see flight as an option and instead, owing to some societal expectation or role responsibility, stay until everyone is out safely. These people shift to fight mode to help others exit. Still others in the room freeze (I always think of the Clash song "Should I Stay or Should I Go"), because they have become temporarily immobilized by fear, which has trumped their flight response. These people often trigger those in fight mode to move for them. We see this phenomenon in footage from crisis situations, where those in fight mode carry or drag out those in freeze mode in whatever way they can.

Although such crises don't often arise in the classroom, students may enter into the same survival mode to manage their stress, manifested by behaviors that can be avoidant, disruptive, or disengaged.

The Julie Scenario

Julie, a 6th grader at the Neighborhood School, is creating quite a ruckus in her 3rd period math class today. She came into the room scowling and has refused to take any notes or even open her book, and the teacher's requests for her attention and eye contact are met only with deeper scowls. Julie has typically been disenchanted with math, and lately her behavior has been especially negative and uncooperative. As Julie's teacher, what do you do?

How It Looks in the Classroom

Julie is a fictitious student, although she probably sounds awfully familiar to most of us. Our classrooms seem to be flooded with student behaviors like Julie's that detract from learning. Students respond to their difficult life situations in a variety of ways, often in the classic survival mode: by withdrawing (flight), acting out (fight), or going numb (freeze). Figure 2.1 shows how these responses usually manifest themselves in the classroom. Keep in mind that this is not meant to be a complete list; every student manages his or her own stress response differently, depending on personal history, genetic makeup, and life experiences.

We have all encountered students in these states. Such responses can derail us from our mission of teaching and transform a classroom atmosphere in seconds. Unruly students, chaotic classrooms, and escalated and disruptive behaviors are not conducive to learning, to put it mildly. When students are in survival mode, the learning environment can suffer tremendously. To quote my friend and colleague Natalie Turner, "Stressed brains can't teach, and stressed brains can't learn." So, we need to increase our awareness of this stress response and be on the lookout for it in our classrooms and other school settings. The sooner we can attune to the motives behind students' behavior and help them identify what it is they really need, the better we'll be able to work with them to identify new ways of coping that are less disruptive to the learning environment and that promote health and learning.

FIGURE 2.1
What Flight, Fight, or Freeze Looks Like in the Classroom

Flight	Fight	Freeze
• Withdrawing • Fleeing the classroom • Skipping class • Daydreaming • Seeming to sleep • Avoiding others • Hiding or wandering • Becoming disengaged	• Acting out • Behaving aggressively • Acting silly • Exhibiting defiance • Being hyperactive • Arguing • Screaming/yelling	• Exhibiting numbness • Refusing to answer • Refusing to get needs met • Giving a blank look • Feeling unable to move or act

How We Typically Respond to the "Julies"

Let's return to Julie. How would you respond to her behavior? What if I gave you a choice? Which of the following five options would you go with?

A. Offer her one more chance to get started on her work; after that, send her to the classroom next door. Her behavior is disruptive to the other students and must not continue like this.

B. Invite her to come to your classroom at lunchtime to talk about math, school, or life, or just to eat. Perhaps she'll open up about what's bothering her.

C. Send her to the office. You will not tolerate disrespectful behavior in your classroom. If she's not ready to learn, she doesn't need to be here.

D. Leave her alone. Focus on your other students who are ready to learn. As long as she's not bothering anyone, she can sit there and scowl.

E. Call a counselor to arrange a parent meeting. You need to get the parents on board ASAP.

Would you have selected one of these, or would you take a different course of action? In my experience, educators usually pick one of the five responses. Here's the thought process behind each:

A. This response demonstrates an expectation that Julie can pull herself together, although you won't extend that opportunity indefinitely. Eventually, you'll have to remove her so that she won't disrupt everyone else's learning.

B. This reflects a willingness to connect with Julie, to build a relationship, and to help the person underneath the behaviors.

C. This demonstrates a mindset that Julie's behaviors require an immediate disciplinary consequence and that through discipline you can change her behaviors.

D. This demonstrates a low expectation for Julie's academic and personal growth and a belief that it isn't worth the time or energy to connect Julie to the learning.

E. This indicates an understanding that Julie needs more help than you can provide in the classroom setting and that perhaps someone else (e.g., a counselor or parents) can help you acquire that support.

Traditionally, most educators have been trained to select A or C, charting a course down a disciplinary path. This path includes removal from class, which may eventually lead to removal from school via suspension or expulsion. We frequently get into power struggles with students like Julie, demanding their immediate response to our instructions—or else. Perhaps we should instead ask, "Is this willful disobedience, or could it be a response to a traumatic life event that Julie is struggling with?"

The Biology of Trauma

When students are in survival mode, their brains are delivering a message that their bodies must respond to. Their behaviors, which are disruptive and often inappropriate, are simply manifestations of what their bodies have been trained to do to survive. Many of these students are, in essence, having normal reactions to not-OK things. In this section, I provide a brief overview of the science behind these responses.

When students are in a state of stress, they are in the part of their brain designed for survival: the limbic area. The limbic system controls arousal, emotion, and the flight, fight, or freeze response. A description I have borrowed from Dr. Dan Siegel, clinical professor of psychiatry at the UCLA School of Medicine, refers to this area as the "downstairs brain." When students' downstairs brains are in charge, their capacity to learn and retain information is disrupted. Our goal is to get them into the higher-functioning part of their brain—the prefrontal cortex—which enables them to think, reason, and maintain flexibility. Siegel (2003) calls this area the "upstairs brain." One of its primary purposes is to *regulate* the downstairs brain—in short, to keep the brain online and to shift into survival mode only when absolutely necessary.

To climb out of survival mode, it is helpful for students to be able to identify the feelings, name the function of their brain, and attune to their biology. This will give them the power to manage the intensity associated with the stress. (In this context, *intensity* refers to the body's stressed state in response to threat.) Often, students experiencing trauma are dealing with situations outside their control and have to manage the stress as best they can. By teaching them about the differences between the upstairs and downstairs brains, we are empowering them to understand their biology and make healthy choices to manage it. I use this model with students, parents, and educators extensively in my practice.

As educators and caregivers, many of us were taught to respond to the behavior in front of us. We learned about developmentally appropriate behaviors and effective classroom management techniques. As a result, many of us associate behaviors with choice. I am now challenging you to look beyond the behavior and focus on *motive*. If we can identify what may be motivating students to react, we can redirect them by providing alternative options for them to manage their stress.

I received the following note from a 1st grade teacher that shows the positive effects this information can have in the classroom:

> It has been so helpful to learn how to teach students about the upstairs and downstairs brain and what that means for learning. I have two students who now use hand signals to show how their brain is feeling on a regular basis. One of my students will self-regulate by putting her own head down and then put her hand up in a *C* shape when she is ready to talk through her frustration. I shared this strategy with her mom at conferences, and the family is using it at home with my student and her brother.
>
> My other student is now able to communicate frustration without throwing his body on the floor and crying. He took a little longer to develop a routine for the brain strategy, but he is now using the routine he developed himself to show when he's feeling frustration.
>
> Both these students are blossoming academically because they are able to deal with their frustrations and move on to enjoy the rest of their day. I am so proud of them!

A school counselor in a Title I school also found this knowledge game-changing:

Having students come up to me in the hallway, and tell me they are not in their "thinking brains" and they are in their "downstairs brains" gives me immediate insight into how a student is feeling. I immediately pull out all my different calming strategies to help coach students back to their "upstairs brains." If a student can learn this at an early age, they are going to be way more prepared for postsecondary education and for a career than someone who does not have these resiliency skills.

What Students Need

Let's return to the saga of Julie. As you might have suspected, this is a more complicated matter than it appeared in the beginning:

Last night, Julie's mom arrived home late, after Julie was supposed to have been in bed. Her mom was drunk, yelled at Julie for being up too late, and then slipped and hurt her arm in the kitchen. Julie retreated to her room, upset and worried—worried because her mom has been drinking more lately, worried that her mom might have really hurt herself, and worried that her mom's relationship with her is withering. Through her own sobs and the wild thoughts running through her head, Julie got about two hours of sleep and left for school before her mom even woke up.

Julie's scenario is sadly not uncommon in today's schools. Students like Julie arrive at school tired, scared, anxious, angry, and overwhelmed by any of a host of events that we refer to as trauma. As we know, the effects on kids can be detrimental, even debilitating.

For years, we have asked students to leave their baggage at the door, to ignore what happened the night or morning before they got to school, and to miraculously enter our settings in the learning mode. We want to keep the outside world separate from our education world, but despite our valiant attempts, it just doesn't work. We cannot separate our lives from our work, so how can we expect those less developmentally advanced to do so?

Many of us do not have the luxury of knowing the details of our students' lives. We don't know what traumatic events our students have endured or what heartache and turmoil they lug to class. We don't know what's on their minds, although we can usually tell when it isn't related to ancient civilizations, algebraic formulas, or this week's vocabulary words.

What students show us is really all they know. It's up to us—the adults in their lives—to offer an array of appropriate, alternative means for them to regulate their emotions and manage the intensity of their behaviors. To do so, we must provide a safe environment in which students are free to explore those strategies, practice them, and discover the ones that work best for them. Just as we do when students struggle with writing a compelling summary or chronicling the events leading up to the Civil War, we must teach students who struggle with managing trauma-related stress. The better we can teach students to recognize when they are in their downstairs brain versus their upstairs brain and give them a tool set for getting back upstairs, the greater the chance we have at supporting students' pursuit of personal and academic success. We may not be able to stop the trauma from happening, but we can give students the skills and strategies to manage the intensity, through intentional teaching in a safe, predictable environment.

Caregiver Self-Awareness: What We Control

Our ultimate goal is to support Julie's academic growth and readiness for long-term success. We want her to learn content and demonstrate skills. Public accountability demands higher assessment scores from her. She must acquire certain grades and pass certain classes to graduate. She must master rigorous course and grade-level standards. And we want her to love learning so that she'll push herself to continue. The fact that her level of achievement may be reflected in our teacher evaluation metrics and that we're attempting to access scarce resources to help her accomplish those goals just adds to our professional stress. To say that teachers' jobs are challenging is a dramatic understatement.

The new challenge is to balance that push for academic success with the overwhelming need to provide all the Julies out there with a safe, trustworthy environment with safe, trustworthy adults caring for them: a trauma-sensitive learning environment.

We know that teacher quality is the number-one school factor determining student success. Educators play a vital role in supporting the healthy development of our students. We have 6, 7, sometimes up to 12 hours a day to teach and supervise our students. What a tremendous opportunity to make a difference! If we are to ensure that our students are healthy, safe, engaged, supported, and challenged, then we must first look at our own contributions to the equation. We play a powerful role in the development and sustainability of trauma-sensitive learning environments, and we have a great deal of influence on the developing mind. How we "set the table" often determines how successful our students will be.

PETE'S PRACTICE

I spent the first half of my career teaching and leading in buildings in which numerous students were struggling, misbehaving, and suffering—and I had no specific plan to address their needs. Not until I met Kristin at a workshop on the effects of trauma did I realize that our precious students had a reason for their vulnerability, and we had options for supporting them.

Immediately, I arranged for Kristin to provide initial training and support to my teaching staffs. There were some early hurdles—teachers' belief systems are often deep-rooted, and habits for responding to student behaviors can be well ingrained—but we stuck with it. With concerted effort, individualized follow-through, frequent reminders, ongoing training by Kristin, and my own work as building principal, we were able to see some significant gains.

The most dramatic data emerged from my assignment as a middle school principal. The student body was high-poverty, with 88 percent of the 600 students qualifying for free or reduced lunch. The school was on the state's Needs Improvement list and had a record of exorbitant disciplinary measures (more than 4,000 office referrals and more than 700 suspensions the year prior to our initial training). We set to work early and often, training teachers in the prevalence of trauma and the effects of living in a constant state of stress. Then we infused strategies for adult self-care and the management of our own emotional well-being as a crucial step in establishing a trauma-sensitive learning environment.

Three years later, discipline referrals were cut in half, suspensions were down 65 percent, and academic growth (as measured by a college-and-career readiness assessment) was up 250 percent. The school culture, once known for its rough-and-tumble attitude and hallway fights, had shifted significantly to one in which learning was the priority. More students were in the learning mode, and our teachers were to credit for this shift. They were in the trenches, they worked directly with our students, and they made the changes necessary for our students to be successful.

Wrapping It Up

Our reactions to student behaviors affect our relationships with those students. The more we are cognizant of our thoughts, emotions, and triggers, the better prepared we'll be to understand our tendencies and patterns of action. Our own self-awareness will prepare us to make healthy choices instead of taking regrettable actions. The overall goal for us is to act with integrity, to be consistent and reliable, to remain logical and regulated in times of stress, and—when facing disruptive, defiant, and disrespectful behavior—to stay in our upstairs brain.

By remaining in control of our own emotions, we are modeling appropriate ways to manage stress. In doing so, we are providing a key component of a trauma-sensitive learning environment. Our students need this from us.

Reflective Questions

1.   Think about some of the student behaviors you observe in your role. Examine them in the context of the flight, fight, or freeze framework. How does this change your thinking, if at all?

2.   After you first read the "Julie Scenario," which of the five responses to her behavior did you lean toward? Why do you suppose that was the case?

3.   After you read further, did you modify your thinking about Julie and your response to her? Why or why not?

4.   Go to https://www.youtube.com/watch?v=gm9CIJ74Oxw and watch Dr. Dan Siegel explain his hand model of the brain. Does this make sense to you?

5.   There is one element of the trauma equation that you can control: yourself. How might you focus on keeping *yourself* in your upstairs brain?

6.   What are some of the major challenges you face in your professional work right now? How are you handling them?

7.   Now that you're armed with research and theory, what is your primary purpose for reading this book? What do you hope to accomplish as you continue reading?

PART II

Self-Awareness

> In the unlikely event of a loss of cabin pressure, oxygen
> masks will fall from the panel above your head. Please
> fasten your own oxygen mask before helping others
> around you.
>
> —Flight attendant at the onset of any airline flight

. . . .

Think about the work you do and the role you play with young people. Regardless of the position or title you hold, your professional responsibilities include providing for the welfare and safety of others. We are in a giving field. The needs of others are our priority, and we often focus so much on what our students, clients, and children need that we overlook our own requirements.

Way back in the day, even before I was born, the famous Greek philosopher Aristotle shared this pertinent and timeless quote: "Knowing yourself is the beginning of all wisdom." It's true. In my clinical practice as a mental health therapist, I devote nearly all my attention to helping my clients uncover the thoughts, beliefs, assumptions, and fears that drive their actions. I often think of myself as an agent of introspection, one who provides a mirror to those who live in a world of windows.

When providing professional development in trauma-sensitive practice to education professionals, my role stays the same. Educators are notorious for giving selflessly, for tending to their students and ignoring their own needs, for buying classroom materials with their own money, and for focusing most of their energy, time, thoughts, and emotions on their students. It is no small feat to get some teachers to even talk about their own needs, let alone address them with action—yet it is a foundational step in the process of becoming a trauma-sensitive practitioner. If we aren't physically, mentally, emotionally, and spiritually healthy, we cannot reasonably expect to be able to help our students become healthier and more successful in school.

Why is this? It's because we're givers. We're altruistic. We don't believe that it should be all about us when our students have such dramatic needs. Self-awareness, self-acceptance, and self-love seem to distract us from our calling to help others. Yet this is actually a short-sighted view that, in the end, will hamper us in our efforts to help our students. Pete reminds me of this line from Shakespeare's *Henry V*: "Self-love, my liege, is not so vile a sin/As self-neglecting." We've got to take care of number one first.

In a trauma-sensitive learning environment, the adult is necessarily in charge of the setting and the tone of the space. It is our demeanor, our approach, our behaviors, our volume, and our presence that affect how our young people live, breathe, and perform in the classroom. When we create a stable, consistent, and safe environment, our students are able to enter and remain in the learning mode. As you'll read in this section, this is when the results of our labor come pouring in (or sometimes just trickling in, but you've got to start somewhere): we can reallocate our time to teaching, our students can focus on learning, and the achievement gains that are required by accountability measures become a reality.

It starts with us. It starts with you.

3

Cement Shoes: Staying True to Who You Are

To be the change we wish to see in the world, we need to be aware of our awareness, to hold within this place of knowing our own unfolding sense of being awake. It requires that we hold our own intention in the front of our minds—that we pay attention to our intention.

—Dan Siegel, professor of psychiatry, UCLA School of Medicine

. . . .

For so many years, we educators have been walking the fine line between making ourselves available to others and holding others accountable. *Availability*, in this sense, refers to our emotional investment, our nurturing and encouragement, and our willingness to engage, empathize, and be there for students as they maneuver through life's many stressors and disappointments. This availability is often seen as a contrast to *accountability*—that is, insisting that students meet certain standards for their learning, behavior, and choices. How to navigate this perceived clash between availability and accountability is the most frequently asked question I receive from educators as they attempt to find the "sweet spot" for supporting students affected by trauma. Complicating matters is the ever-present pressure of the ticking clocks, the high expectations for learning, and our own competing professional responsibilities.

In such an environment, it's easy to see why teacher stress and attrition are so high. It's crucial, therefore, that teachers not brush aside self-care as an unnecessary luxury; on the contrary, taking care of ourselves is what enables us to take care of our students.

The Importance of Self-Care

Those of us in the caregiving field ironically tend to have the hardest time walking the walk in this area: we know what we should be doing to take care of ourselves, yet we struggle mightily with carrying it out. Educators stay at work late and sacrifice time on the weekends to ensure that they are meeting the needs of their charges. Those I work with e-mail me late at night or on the weekends. I often find myself replying, "You work too much!" or "Go be with your family!"

We have to set a realistic goal of what we can do, even if we feel like we are always being asked to jump higher, do more, or try harder. The constant stress of not feeling good enough begins to weigh heavily on our hearts and overall motivation levels. It is also a quick journey to burnout, a place where no one wants to end up. So reflect on these questions: what will most likely ensure your ability to stay in this field? What will most likely contribute to your health and balance? What can you do to avoid entering into the dreaded state of burnout? Self-care isn't just about bubble baths: on a deeper level, it's about staying connected to ourselves and being true to who we are and how we want to be.

Be True to You

One thing I have learned is that the more self-aware we become, the easier it is for us to manage the needs of those in front of us. We are most likely to make mistakes or say things we regret when we venture away from our sense of self. Begin to imagine and define what your true sense of self looks like. Often, as my clients leave their session, I say, "Be true to you." This resonates for so many that one of my clients even made me a necklace with that very saying on it. She talks often of how that phrase supports her in her decisions as a medical professional and helps her maintain balance in her personal life. As you begin to define your sense of self, think about which key aspects of yourself cannot, no matter what, be taken from you. What can you truly hold on to and rely on? The answers become your way of identifying your *cement shoes*.

Mental imagery helps bring this metaphor to life. Imagine that you're walking on the beach toward the ocean. When you are up to your ankles in the water and a wave hits, what happens? What about when you are up to your knees, waist, or chest? The farther you go out, the more likely you are to be toppled by the waves that crash upon you.

Now I would like you to imagine that you have on a pair of cement shoes. If you were firmly grounded where you stood, you would be less likely to be toppled by the waves that hit you, no matter how big. Although I would never recommend that anyone stand in the ocean wearing cement shoes, I want you to envision this as a way of staying true—to your ideals, integrity, vision, beliefs, and self—in your classroom or other professional setting.

Students and their families come at us in many challenging ways. From the little ripples to the larger swells and breakers, they present to us a variety of stressors and levels of intensity that can throw us off balance. How can we stay true to who we are and ensure that no matter what hits us, we will stay faithful to our internal identity? This is what I am asking you to do in your work with students and families: define your cement shoes and keep them on. If you do this, you will be less likely to be swayed from who you are and how you want to be, and you will be less likely to compromise yourself and your integrity in the process.

Ms. London, Kelly, and the Power of Cement Shoes

Ms. London has been teaching at the local high school for five years. She is passionate about the work she does with her students and is highly motivated to ensure that they are as successful as possible. She developed her personal mission statement as a first-year teacher. Although she has made some edits to it over the years, the themes have been consistent. Her mission statement helps ground her each morning, and she refers to it often throughout the day, especially before some of her more difficult classes. Posted near her desk was a beautifully handwritten copy: "My mission is to motivate all students to learn, to believe in the best in everyone, to find the strengths in all students, to be known as a safe and caring educator, and to challenge each student to be the best he or she can be."

In her 4th period class, Ms. London had a 10th grader named Kelly. Ms. London knew very little about Kelly, although she had overheard her talking about avoiding home and staying with friends. Kelly had a history of suspensions and was known as a "troublemaker" among the other teachers. She was so notorious for her disruptions, in fact, that many teachers had started to allow her to have her way just to avoid a scene. Ms. London would hear them in the teachers' lounge saying things like, "I just want to make it through class without an incident." In Ms. London's class, Kelly's disruptions often distracted other students from learning.

One day, Ms. London became so frustrated that in front of the whole class she said, "Kelly, for once can you just knock it off and focus on the lesson? I am so sick of your distractions and disrespect. If you can't pull it together, then don't bother coming to class." The whole room fell silent. Kelly appeared shocked by this outburst and then screamed, "Fine! Screw you, anyway. I'm out of here!" And Kelly left the class, slamming the door behind her.

Later, Ms. London asked herself, *Is that what I really wanted for Kelly or for the class? Did my outburst accomplish anything positive? How can I fix this mess?* She realized that she had violated several statements from her mission statement. She had not motivated Kelly to connect with her learning, she had not focused on Kelly's strengths, and she had not presented herself as a safe and caring educator.

In the heat of the moment, Ms. London had kicked off her cement shoes. With the prospect of Kelly (hopefully) returning to class the next day, Ms. London needed a game plan. She decided to take two steps that would align with her mission statement: she would *repair* (see Chapter 6 for more on repairing) with Kelly, and she would create a *plan for taking a break* as necessary.

First, the repair: the next day, Ms. London approached Kelly privately and asked if she would stay after class. Kelly agreed. When class was over, Ms. London said, "Kelly, I want to apologize for my angry outburst, my frustration, and what I said to you in class yesterday. I had no right to say those things to you in front of the class. I am truly sorry. I put you in an unfair position, and I don't blame you for leaving." Kelly was listening, warily.

Ms. London continued, "I think you are a great kid. I think you are smart and that you have a lot of potential. I get frustrated at times when you don't seem to work to your potential, and when you distract the class. I don't know a lot about you—what interests you, what you want for your life. I *do* know that I want you to be a successful student in my class. I will make the commitment to keep checking in with you and not to act like that again. I am asking that you make the commitment to come to my class and try to focus on learning. Does that sound fair?" Kelly nodded and agreed to give it a try.

Next, the plan for taking a break: Ms. London had realized that this wasn't the first time she had acted out of emotion, and it wouldn't be the last. She recognized that she was human, she made mistakes, and it was important to learn from them. In angry and tense moments, it's best for one or the other party to call a time-out and take a break. Ms. London proposed this to Kelly, and they agreed on a signal that would prompt them to step away from each other until cooler heads could prevail.

Although things did not get better overnight, they did improve. Ms. London did not let the fear of another outburst interfere with strengthening her relationship with Kelly. She was also eventually able to help Kelly understand how her choices disrupted not only her own learning but also the learning of others, and she began to work with Kelly on finding a different way of managing her stress. Most important, by repairing and creating a plan with Kelly, Ms. London was able to "re-cement" to her true self, growing closer to fulfilling her personal mission statement. By modeling her vulnerability, she fostered Kelly's growth and ability to handle stress. She had put her cement shoes back on.

Mission: Possible

We can start to define our cement shoes by creating our own personal mission statement. Successful businesses and organizations do this to clarify their purpose, so why can't individuals do the same? When we get a clear understanding of what our mission is, it becomes easier for us to stay true to it. Our mission statement clarifies our core values, our unifying purpose—our true north. When we stay grounded in our truth, we not only serve as a role model for those students who are just setting out to define themselves but also will be less likely to compromise our integrity. We will behave and interact in ways that make us feel proud, not remorseful.

In my practice, I use this exercise to support professionals who have become lost because of burnout or trauma history, but it can be monumentally helpful to all of us. It rededicates us to our work, reaffirms our inner selves, and helps us define our own trigger points and areas of contention. Further, it gives us something tangible to hold on to and reflect on during those times when we are feeling most compromised and vulnerable.

Take a moment and think about how you would like to be seen and interpreted. Here's another way to look at it: if your students were to give you a tribute speech, what would you want it to include? How would you like them to describe you? There is no single answer here; each of us must figure out our own "fit." Being true to ourselves means accepting ourselves for who we are, not who others wish we could be (or how we imagine others would like us to be). Acting in ways that align with our knowledge of ourselves will ensure a more cohesive and consistent response in all arenas of our job—with students, families, and fellow staff and in stressful and not-so-stressful situations—an essential ingredient for trauma-sensitive practice. Attempting to act in a manner that is not true to ourselves, on the other hand, sets the stage for mistrust and disruption.

Your Turn

I have seen firsthand how transformational the process of developing a personal mission statement is. Now it's time to create your own. The following questions provide a good jumping-off point. Typically, as you complete the exercise, one or two key themes emerge as the foundation of who you are and how you want to be. What do you think your overarching theme or message would be? The results may reaffirm what you already believe about yourself or surprise you with what they reveal.

- What do you love?

- Why did you choose this profession?

- Why do you continue to go to work every day?

- Whom do you seek out as a partner in your career/life?

- What is your inspiration behind teaching?

- Where do you lead others?

- What would you like to accomplish in your career/life?

- What do you believe about students?

- What are three core values that are important to you?

- What three words would you like others to use to describe you at your retirement dinner?

You can add in a few questions of your own. I recommend that you not think too hard at the start of this and just write down what comes to mind. Get out that initial response, and then give yourself permission to reflect and edit. If you really want to challenge yourself, once you have completed the exercise, find a safe and trusted person and read your answers aloud. You can even have your partner do this exercise with you.

The next step is to bring these initial notes together into a cohesive mission statement, or at least a working draft of one. Feel free to update and revise it as often as you like.

 Based on your responses to the questions in the previous exercise, write a statement that encapsulates what drives you. What are your cement shoes?

PETE'S PRACTICE

At one of the elementary schools I led, I worked alongside a veteran 6th grade teacher named Mrs. O'Connor who was known for having a big heart. Although our school was located in a rough neighborhood with high poverty, high transience, and an extraordinarily high rate of incarcerated parents, Mrs. O'Connor was committed to making her classroom a safe haven for her students. She often commented to me that her calling was to make every day as wonderful as it could possibly be.

It was no surprise, then, that her mission statement was this clear: "To give my students the best shot at learning, I'll make sure each and every day is a brand-new, blank-slate day."

To be sure, she had challenging students who put this mission statement to the test. One of the primary challenges arrived in the form of a young man named Channing. Good-looking, smart, and resourceful, Channing had a way of irritating his teachers and manipulating situations to get out of work. He also used his interpersonal skills to recruit other students to do his homework, confess to his misdeeds, and stir up a ruckus. On more than one occasion, his shenanigans landed him in after-school detention, and on one occasion, he leapt out of the second-story window to avoid his hour-long confinement.

It would have been easy to raise our hands in resignation and banish him from class. That response was par for the course with Channing: by 6th grade, he had already accumulated quite a log of out-of-school suspensions. However, Mrs. O'Connor wouldn't allow that. Every time Channing erupted in class, coerced a classmate into lying, or otherwise misbehaved, she would refer the behavior to the office and then insist that she have a chance to talk with the young man.

Every conversation began the same way: "Channing, I know that [*misbehavior*] happened. I don't know why, and I don't know what your consequence in the office is going to be for it. However, I want you to know this: our classroom is a safe place, and it's got to be safe for everyone. I'm going to take this incident and throw it into the Sea of Forgetfulness. When you earn your way back into class, which I hope happens really quickly, we'll get right back to learning, and we'll move forward. We're not going to dredge up old memories or rehash old behaviors. You get a fresh start, because your learning is that important, and because you are that important. I won't let anything—even your own behaviors—get in the way of your learning."

The Sea of Forgetfulness. What an amazing concept. To the students in Mrs. O'Connor's class, that was a very real place, and it must have harbored hundreds of transgressions and even a couple of crimes. That Mrs. O'Connor pledged to toss each wrongdoing into it and lived up to her end of the bargain spoke volumes to her students.

And, over the year, it spoke volumes to Channing. As the weeks passed, he settled into a relatively stable, predictable routine. He worked hard in Mrs. O'Connor's classes and even mentioned her in his 6th grade promotion speech. He still managed to get into a little trouble here and there, but his learning, on which Mrs. O'Connor placed a premium, indeed became his focus. He, like all the students in Mrs. O'Connor's class, started each day with a fresh canvas—thanks to Mrs. O'Connor staying in her cement shoes.

Wrapping It Up

One of the hardest things we have to face as professionals is the fact that we often do not know what traumatic events our students have experienced. We cannot stop the not-OK from happening to them, and we have little influence over how our students respond to their not-OK circumstances. Although we can't "fix" the issues that present themselves to us, however, we can stay true to ourselves and the kinds of educators we want to be. By modeling that intentionality, humility, strength, honesty, and grace, we can provide opportunities for others to begin to do that for themselves. Life is messy, and identifying our sense of self—in the form of cement shoes—helps us "manage the mess." Our ability to be consistent and resolute, acting in congruence with our personal mission statements, enables us to support our students by being available to them while holding them accountable. That is far more valuable to our students and families than we may ever know.

Reflective Questions

1. What were your first thoughts when you read the chapter title? How did your thinking about the phrase "cement shoes" change as you learned more about its meaning?

2. Think for a moment about the concept of self-care. Do you devote much time to your own health and well-being? Why or why not?

3. Think of a couple of ways in which you can "take care of number one" on a regular basis. Phrase your responses in a way that demonstrates that this will support your professional growth and your service to others, not interfere with them.

4. What are your core values? List them on a sheet of paper. How do they relate to your professional responsibilities?

5. What was the mission-statement exercise like for you? What did you gain from engaging in it?

6.   What did you learn (or what have you reaffirmed) about yourself through the mission-statement exercise? Did any themes emerge as a result?

7.   What are your plans to keep the mission statement prominent in your mind as you work and grow? What do you intend to do with it in the long run?

4

Stay Out of Oz: Remaining Grounded Amid Chaos

Not realizing that children exposed to inescapable, overwhelming stress may act out their pain, that they may misbehave, not listen to us, or seek our attention in all the wrong ways, can lead us to punish these children for their misbehavior.... If only we knew what happened last night, or this morning before he/she got to school, we would be shielding the same child we're now reprimanding.

—Mark Katz, *Playing a Poor Hand Well*

For children and their caregivers, living with chronic stress and trauma can be challenging, to say the least. It is not uncommon for children to cope by stirring up chaos in their environment. This is not an intentional attempt to hurt others; rather, it is the best tool they've got to manage the intensity of their reality. Children learn early on, either consciously or unconsciously, ways to stay safe, to attempt to control their surroundings, and to manage their stress levels.

Recall from Chapter 2 our discussion of the upstairs and downstairs brains. When children are feeling stress, their brains go downstairs. Our brains were designed to be downstairs, or limbic-controlled, only for short periods—for survival. Once there, the brain operates in the flight, fight, or freeze framework until the crisis is over and then reverts to the normal mode. Students who experience chronic stress and trauma, however, *live* in their downstairs brain.

Our goal is to help students understand what their bodies' biological responses are when they are in the midst of overwhelming stress, to give them the tools and strategies to override their tendencies to go (or stay) "downstairs," and to work with them to stay "upstairs"—responding logically, thoughtfully, and intentionally to the reality they're facing.

When we start to think of students' misbehavior as an attempt to manage intensity, it gives us a broader and more understandable focus to work with. Many of us were trained to take behavior at face value and to respond accordingly. But what if we went beyond a surface-level interpretation and challenged ourselves to look at what is *motivating* the behaviors? Understanding the motive is the path to true change.

Beware of Tornadoes

Just like poor Dorothy in *The Wonderful Wizard of Oz*, we sometimes find ourselves seized by a tornado—that is, caught in the tumult created by a student throwing a tantrum, acting out, "exploding," or otherwise disrupting the learning environment. Although it causes disequilibrium for us as adults and caregivers, the tornado itself is simply the student's effort to manage the intensity of his or her situation. The motivation is often clear: the disruption takes the focus away from self and the discomfort of the current circumstances. Many of us can think of a student or a family member who has learned to live this way. Sometimes it seems as though they thrive on chaos.

Kids growing up in a chronic "state of alert" have learned early on to take cues from their environment. They watch those around them—parents, teachers, other adults, and other children—to identify the strategies people use to manage stress. Often, constructing a "tornado" is just a learned tactic of avoiding the truth. For instance, a student who is struggling in a particular academic area, such as reading, might cause a ruckus to avoid having to join the reading group. This student's uncomfortable "truth" is that he struggles with reading, and his response is to dodge it by whatever means he has at his disposal. Being compelled to read is the *trigger*—the factor that causes a stress response—and the tornado becomes the escape mechanism, effectively rescuing him from a stressful situation by either stimulating his own regulation (because being in the downstairs brain is more comfortable and manageable) or creating bedlam for others to deal with (in this case, his teacher).

The tornado is simply a distraction. Our goals, as professionals, are to stay focused on the task, to stay grounded in the truth, and to avoid getting sucked into the tornado and taken to Oz. Not only do we want to help the student see how his body is responding and how he can head off his own tornado, but we must also maintain our own sense of control. Our ability to stay in our upstairs brain in this moment ensures a stable, calm environment for ourselves, for the other students watching this spectacle, and for the instigating student, who needs to be able to access the alternative coping strategies he has learned. If we succumb to our downstairs brain, the chaos spreads, we "flip our lids," and the intent of the distraction is fulfilled: the student doesn't have to read.

The Upstairs Brain Prevails

Take a moment and think about a time when you had an incredible conversation with a student, parent, or colleague and were able to connect on a higher level—personally, professionally, emotionally, spiritually, grammatically. You and this other person were "in the zone" together. As you reflect on this experience, I hope you are also able to remember that you *self-acknowledged* when that conversation was over—that is, you found a way to congratulate or honor yourself for your ability to make that connection. Such an interaction is an example of two upstairs brains working together toward something positive. In reality, you have many of these interactions throughout your day; you often just don't give yourself credit for them.

Now I want you to think of a time when you completely blew it with a student, parent, or colleague. Most likely, this experience still haunts you. In the heat of the moment, you engaged in a verbal argument, exchanged words that you regret, did something hurtful, or otherwise behaved in a way incongruous with your true self and values, and the situation became so overwhelming that you still feel stunned when you think about it. Not to worry; this has happened to all of us. Sometimes these exchanges occur so spontaneously that we still aren't sure how they got to that point. Such interactions are examples of two downstairs brains colliding, sometimes with catastrophic consequences.

Let's shift gears. Can you recall a time when a student, parent, or colleague came to you looking for a fight? Guns drawn, dukes up, in full attack mode, this person wanted a piece of your hide! Possibly snarling at or insulting you or being physically aggressive, this individual was clearly in his or her downstairs brain. Perhaps you don't even know why this person was so upset, why his or her emotional response obliterated his or her ability to think rationally. Was this a comfortable spot for you? Of course not! But we don't always have the luxury of knowing what will trigger a tornado; all we know is that it happens.

The challenge for us is to avoid getting sucked into the tornado and being whisked off to Oz. Our job, instead, is to stand outside the tornado and encourage the instigator back into Kansas. Put another way, we have to stay in our upstairs brain and help the other person come back upstairs to join us.

PETE'S PRACTICE

As a middle school principal, I had frequent interactions with Deron, an 8th grade student who was prone to causing tornadoes in every classroom he entered. From the first day of school, his outbursts and dramatic entrances in many of his classes spun his classmates—and his teacher—right into the tornado with him. Invariably, he ended up outside my office with a discipline referral in his hand or torn up on the floor.

In his American History class, however, things were different. Mr. Trout, his teacher, refused to engage in an argument or confrontation about Deron's unruly behavior. Instead, Mr. Trout enacted three strategies to mitigate the effect of Deron's daily tornado: first, he facilitated discussions with the class about each person's unique ability to handle life's stressors and our collective need for consistency and grace. Second, he organized his classroom so that the entry task was always posted, so that students could enter and begin their work immediately. Third, he would calmly wait out Deron's tirade, connect with him with a comment such as "I'm sorry last period was tough on you. I'm glad you're here today! Let me know if you need help getting your entry task squared away," and then move to another spot in the classroom.

Although Deron had come to expect the heave-ho to the office for his behaviors (perhaps meeting a "flight" response), he gradually came to accept the reality that Mr. Trout wasn't going to banish him, he could get help if he needed it, and this room was a safe place for him.

Michael's Story

Michael is in 4th grade and tends to create tornadoes in the classroom. He has been known to take things out of others' hands, push classmates, create distractions by acting silly or talking back to the teacher, or just flat-out refuse to do any work. One of Michael's least favorite things to do is math. Math has been a struggle for him for years, as he has always had difficulty understanding number relationships and equations. He often loses patience with himself and rips up his paper. Other students in the class know that he hates math.

The three other students seated at Michael's table are known to the class as the "rule followers." They require the least amount of attention from their teacher, Ms. Jones, so she can shift her focus to the others in the classroom who are more in need of 1:1 attention. Ms. Jones strategically placed Michael with them in hopes that they would support Michael in making healthy choices.

One day, after Ms. Jones handed out the math assignment, Michael grinned, grabbed his tablemates' papers, wadded them up, and tossed them toward the garbage can.

Take a moment and reflect: what do you imagine the "rule followers" did in response to Michael's actions?

Of course, they immediately went to their own downstairs brains. They said, "Michael, give them back!" Michael's response was to laugh, mocking them for not being able to do their work. This caused further disruption, and within minutes, the table was yelling for the teacher.

Take another moment to reflect: how do you think Ms. Jones responded to this situation?

Unfortunately, she also went downstairs. She became visibly upset, walked over to Michael's table, and ordered him to get his tablemates' papers and pull himself together. When he initially refused to budge, she raised her voice and issued an ultimatum: "Michael, get the papers or leave the room."

In a matter of moments, the once-promising math lesson had crumbled. The confrontation with Michael captured the attention of the entire class, and students who typically were able to regulate became dysregulated. Soon enough, nobody was focused on the assigned task. Safety and security were out the window, students were going into a heightened state of alert, and math became an afterthought.

This is a classic example of a tornado. Michael managed his own distress at the prospect of doing the assigned task by creating a diversion. His disruption resulted in classroom chaos and a showdown with his teacher, who joined him in a confrontation of downstairs brains. Together, they traveled to Oz. You can probably cite your own examples of tornadoes that you have witnessed in your own classroom.

Be the Good Witch!

We've established that the goal for all of us is to avoid getting sucked into these tornadoes, but how? The first step is monitoring our own regulation. It is imperative that we are able to know our own set of triggers and see them for what they are. It's OK to admit it; we *all* have triggers. The key is to acknowledge them and learn to manage them in healthy ways—while staying in our cement shoes.

One way we can begin to do this is to focus on the truth. When a tornado hits, we ask ourselves, *What is happening in front of me? What is the student really asking for? What might be motivating him or her to make these choices?*

In addition, we must take the time to acknowledge our emotions and our biological responses to this situation by asking, *How am I feeling about this student and this behavior? How can I respond in a way that supports this student instead of reacting emotionally to his or her choices? What do I need at this time to stay focused on the needs of the student?*

Another important key is to focus on whom we are working with. Because we work in a service-oriented profession, it is imperative that we direct our attention externally, to help address our students' immediate needs. To be successful in a classroom, we must know our students well, build strong relationships with them, and connect with them often. Knowing their personalities, habits, strengths, and fears will support the creation of a trauma-sensitive learning environment. The more we are in touch with our students, the more effectively we can formulate healthy responses and intervention techniques.

Think back to the scenario in Michael's math class. What was the point at which Ms. Jones could have redirected this entire incident? One defining moment was when the students called her over to their table after Michael pitched their papers. She could have stayed out of the tornado entirely and addressed the situation like this: "Michael, I can see you're frustrated about doing math today. Not to worry; we're all here to help make sure you learn today's concepts. In fact, I'll be stopping by your table first to make sure you all understand how to do this. Will you please pick up those papers so we can get started?"

An Ounce of Prevention

Handling a tornado responsibly and intentionally in the heat of the moment is one thing. Anticipating it and preparing a plan beforehand in an attempt to *avoid* it is another strategy altogether. As I have always said in my professional practice and personal life, if it's predictable, it's preventable.

In this case, we already know of Michael's troubles with math. We also know that his tendency, when triggered, is to disrupt his immediate environment. Thus, we can assume that there is a strong likelihood that he will have a visible and audible reaction to being given a math assignment. If we are to prevent the tornado and create a positive, safe environment for Michael and his classmates, what should we do? How can we support Michael in showing a healthy response to the assignment versus a triggered reaction? Several strategies can help, as Ms. Jones learned. As the school year went on, she began to

- **Prepare Michael for the beginning of math class.** She maintained a regular routine with consistent structures, so he knew what time math class would be starting and when he could expect to get an assignment.
- **Make a habit of supporting his learning.** She made his table the first stop on her trip around the room to provide timely feedback. She circulated back to his table often, checking in to make sure he was doing well. When this became the routine, he knew it wouldn't be too long before he got help.
- **Provide training and support in peer tutoring and cooperative learning.** When students saw one another as part of their support networks, they didn't have to rely on the teacher as much.
- **Involve Michael in the operation of the classroom.** She assigned him a specific role each day—like passing out the worksheets or sharpening pencils—to help him feel involved and part of the process, so the math assignment wouldn't feel like something that was being done *to* him.

Each of the steps listed above is *proactive*. All too often, we wait for the tornado to hit and then *react*. Implementing healthy intervention strategies beforehand diverts our students' reactionary responses, equips them with appropriate options, and intercepts the tornado.

Now let's approach this from the educator's standpoint. What happens when you have to interact with a tornado? What if tornadoes tend to happen on a regular basis? What support do you need from others? What would help you better manage the stress and emotion associated with working with students who struggle? What strategies can you use to keep yourself out of Oz in these moments? Ms. Jones worked diligently to maintain her composure by

- **Having a plan.** She studied her in-class discipline data and determined her problem areas. Then she created a plan to prevent problems in these areas and simultaneously wrote down how she would approach any outbursts or arguments that did arise.

- **Avoiding power struggles.** Ms. Jones made a pledge to avoid power struggles, and she shared this with her students. She committed to sharing class expectations, being consistent, and allowing students to make their own choices. These actions became part of their classroom routine.
- **Knowing the students.** By building strong relationships with her students, she was able to determine what motivated them, connected them to their learning, and refocused them. Getting to know their parents, too, strengthened this essential bond.
- **Reinforcing the goal to stay out of Oz.** For Ms. Jones, this included putting up a *Wizard of Oz* movie poster in the back of the room. The students didn't know what it represented, but Ms. Jones used it as a physical reminder of this strategy.

Wrapping It Up

Despite our best intentions, Oz happens. Students, parents, colleagues, and supervisors can unleash a tornado right in front of us, and it's our choice to get sucked into it or to stay out of Oz. By staying grounded, engaging in proactive behaviors, and responding with a plan, we can stay emotionally regulated. This benefits our students *and* us. So, when you find yourself being sucked into Oz, remember to tap those ruby slippers and remind yourself, "There's no place like home, there's no place like home, there's no place like home." Or at least upstairs.

Reflective Questions

1. Think of a time when you were faced with a tornado. How did you feel? How did you respond?

2. Have you ever been sucked into someone else's tornado? What caused this? Why did you make the decision to go to Oz? Was it intentional?

3. Consider a student you know who tends to create chaos. Think carefully about when and where this happens. Now try to determine the motive behind it.

4. What does this student need from you to regulate and move back into his or her upstairs brain?

5. What strategies have worked with this student in the past when he or she has "tornadoed" the entire room? What has *not* worked? Can you identify a pattern here? What is it?

6. When one student causes a ruckus, it affects others. What has worked to bring the whole class back in line? How can you prepare students to handle a classmate's tornado?

7. What supports do you need to stay in your own upstairs brain and not get triggered into a reaction to someone else's tornado?

5

When in Doubt, Shut Your Mouth and Take a Breath

> Your breathing is your greatest friend. Return to it in all your troubles and you will find comfort and guidance.
>
> —Buddhist proverb

. . . .

Have you ever really paid attention to your breathing? Most of us are relatively unaware of the continuous expansion and contraction of our airflow, and few of us have ever learned the skill of true deep breathing. Most of us are shallow breathers, taking in enough oxygen to sustain our bodies but not enough to significantly fuel them. Breathing is a process that does more than just sustain us; in fact, strategic breathing approaches can amplify the quality of our health, our learning, and our interactions.

More to the point, we need to truly breathe to regulate our bodies. Our self-regulation ability is crucial to our jobs and to our interactions with students and their families. By regulating our bodies, we stay in our upstairs brain, which enables us to connect with and respond to the needs of our students.

Just Breathe

I have found the following exercise, called "peekaboo" breathing, useful for adults and children alike; I've used it to help little ones as young as 2 learn how to breathe correctly. Try it, and see how it strengthens your skill in deep breathing:

> Grab a small stuffed animal and lie down on your back on the floor. Place the stuffed animal on your stomach so that it rests stably. Now, breathe in deeply and slowly so that the stuffed animal rises with your belly. Continue to inhale until you can make eye contact with the little fellow. Hold your breath in for a moment, and then slowly exhale, allowing the stuffed critter to lower slowly with your belly. As the animal rises, you can say, "Peekaboo!", which the early learning population seems to love, or you can think of it as a slow and methodical means of having your stuffed animal do a push-up. It is best to perform this exercise 10 times in a row.

After you complete this exercise, how does your body feel? Do you notice a shift in your mood? Are you calmer? Do you feel more relaxed? Has some of your anxiety or tension been alleviated? That is the intention: you have enabled your body to calm down and to regulate. I did this with my son one night when he was 4, and he fell asleep before he got to eight. Now that he's almost 9, we still do this when he needs it. The oxygen filling our bodies gives our brains permission to send a signal indicating that we are "safe" and there is no need to be in the flight, fight, or freeze mode, where many of us have learned to dwell.

Teaching students and ourselves to breathe deeply is key in helping us all access—and stay in—our upstairs brain. Deep breathing is particularly crucial before such tasks as eating, transitioning to a new topic, taking a test, or preparing for a change in the schedule. Having students pay attention to the difference in their breathing when they are regulated (in their upstairs brain) and when they are dysregulated (in their downstairs brain) will help them become aware of how their bodies act differently in each of these states and how that affects their capacity to learn. Deep breathing can serve as a tremendous resource in helping them maintain or, when needed, return to a regulated state. Besides peekaboo breathing, you can do yoga with your students, body awareness exercises, body scans, guided imagery, storytelling, music exercises, brain breaks, or something you have created yourself. Take some time to research these options and brainstorm how you can integrate them into your practice.

Breathing and Self-Control: Using the "Pause" Button

In my readings, I stumbled upon a quotation from Viktor Frankl's (1997) *Man's Search for Meaning*: "Between stimulus and response there is space, and in that space lies our power and our freedom." I find it inspiring that although we, and many of our students, do not have control over the adversities that affect our lives and our physiologies, we do possess an element of control over how we respond to our circumstances.

One method of harnessing that control is through our breathing, which enables us to regulate and calm ourselves and access our upstairs brain. It's time to give ourselves and our students the opportunity to pause and reflect before reacting to whatever is happening in front of us. That moment of deliberate thought, that instant of calming, those few seconds of breathing can make all the difference between a cata-strophic emotional reaction and an intentional, rational response. To help you prepare for these challenging moments, just think of the say-ing, "When in doubt, shut your mouth and take a breath."

That simple piece of advice is a "pause" button for our decision-making processes. If we give our students and ourselves the gift of the pause button, how many "lid flips" do you think we can prevent? Although none of us is perfect—there will still be times when we descend to our downstairs brain—the more we pause, the closer we get to creating and sustaining a safe environment to nurture our students' development.

When we live, learn, or work in an environment wrought with chronic stress or trauma, we are less likely to connect our emotions with our thoughts. In such situations, we typically learn either to think through things and avoid feelings entirely or to let our emotions drive our responses and act in ways that we regret. By giving ourselves per-mission to breathe before we act and to allow our thoughts and emo-tions to connect, we are more apt to make an intentional choice instead of a reactionary one.

When we're in our downstairs brain, we often say or do things we later wish we hadn't. After we've calmed down to a regulated state, we can think of all sorts of more appropriate paths we could have taken. What if we could pause sooner and access those options when they'd be most useful—in the heat of the moment?

Baselines and Triggers

How do we equip our students and ourselves with the ability to press the pause button? There are two steps: (1) increasing our awareness of our own baseline energy and (2) identifying the triggers that send us to our downstairs brain.

Determining our baseline energy level. Our individual *baseline energy*—the way we typically feel and present ourselves—is determined by our temperament, attitude, and life experiences. When we can home in on our baseline energy level and acknowledge how it feels, we are better able to detect when that baseline is disrupted. Recognizing our baseline energy level also enables us to understand and accept the energy levels of those around us.

Think about your own baseline energy level. Are you typically a high-energy or a low-energy person? Do you identify more with Tigger or Eeyore from *Winnie-the-Pooh*, or would you describe yourself as someone more even-keeled? How might other people describe your energy level? When you hit that "flow"—when everything seems to be clicking and you're feeling good—what are you doing? How active are you during your best moments? Journaling your responses to questions like these can help you gain awareness of your baseline energy level, so you'll know how you ought to feel when things are going well.

Identifying triggers. Once we identify our baseline energy level, we can start to pay attention to what shifts us off of it and disrupts our regulation. Sometimes this happens unexpectedly, but most often, we can identify certain stimuli that trigger the disruption to our energy level.

Triggers occur all the time—some positive, some negative. It's the negative triggers that send us to our downstairs brain, so it's vital for us to identify and learn to manage them. There are several common stimuli or states that make us more susceptible to being thrown off-kilter:

• **Exhaustion.** When we don't get enough sleep or are generally worn out, we tend to have less patience, energy, and tolerance for disruption. We can all probably think of a time when we had to apologize for something we said or did when we were extremely tired.

• **Previous bad experiences.** When we've gone through something stressful or traumatic, encountering a similar circumstance may trigger us. Think of food poisoning: there are certain foods I refuse to eat because in the past I spent several hours on the bathroom floor re-tasting them. Our history can provide rational or irrational triggers.

- **Challenges to our belief system.** Someone challenging a deeply held belief can serve as an emotional trigger. Debates over such charged topics as religion, politics, student discipline, and even homework policies can cause people to expend quite a bit of emotional energy.

- **Preconceived notions.** When we have a rigid expectation of how people should behave, what should happen, or who should be doing something, and that expectation isn't met, it can be a source of stress for us. For educators, things often don't go as planned, so this is a common trigger.

- **Fear.** The two words that arguably create the greatest disequilibrium in humans are "What if?" When facing the unknown, we often conjure images of dreadful, unpleasant scenarios. Even if we know that such events are extremely unlikely to occur, we may still fear the possibility, setting us up for an intense reaction.

The following "Pete's Practice" will lead you through an exercise to identify your own personal triggers.

PETE'S PRACTICE

One of my former colleagues, Rachel, was a marvelous middle school English teacher. Among the attributes that most impressed me was her utterly unflappable demeanor. After a particularly hectic day, during which several troublesome students had been sent to her classroom to "refocus," I connected with Rachel to try to extract the cause of her calmness.

As it turns out, her philosophy is simple, and it's echoed by Kristin in her trainings: "If it's predictable, it's preventable." In an education context, that saying is usually about student misbehaviors and our ability to cut them off at the pass. In this case, however, Rachel was referring to her own responses to the chaos of middle school.

"Nothing a middle schooler does can surprise me anymore," she said. "Not that I've seen it all or anything, but I'm always expecting the unexpected. When the weirdness starts, I just smile and try to figure it out with them!"

Rachel's invigorating mindset got me thinking, so I worked with Kristin to create the following activity that aims to help you identify your triggers and proactive ways to deal with them.

Ideal Student Behaviors and Attributes	Least Favorite Student Behaviors and Attributes

How do you typically respond to your least favorite student behaviors and attributes (i.e., your triggers)?

What are some more appropriate ways you could respond to your triggers?

Take out a piece of paper and fold it in half, creating two columns (or use the table above, also available as a downloadable form). In the left-hand column (column 1), write down the behaviors and attributes of your ideal student. Record all the things that make you feel excited to come to school each day. If names of students pop into your head as you complete this activity, great! Take a moment to appreciate them and reinforce your love for your job. With a class full of these students, you could teach forever!

In the right-hand column (column 2), write down the behaviors and attributes of your least favorite type of student, including the characteristics, attitudes, and scenarios that frustrate and irritate you. These are the things that make you want to press the "snooze" button on your alarm clock and scout for non-education-related jobs online. Specific students may appear on this list, too.

Now compare the two lists. Pay close attention to the feelings you associate with the descriptors in each list. Remember: no feelings are bad; they are all healthy and necessary. Completing this activity gives you permission to validate how you truly feel when faced with particular circumstances, individuals, and behaviors. This process is crucial to developing your sense of self and identifying your triggers.

Column 2 is the beginning of a list of your negative triggers. Write down how you typically react to the behaviors, actions, or scenarios you've listed in column 2. (Note: you could do the same for column 1 to see what responses your joy-enhancing triggers elicit.) As you proceed, you might see a trend developing. What do you notice? Do your reactions stem from your upstairs brain or your downstairs brain? Next, for each of the triggers in column 2, write an appropriate response that you could make. If you were to truly shut your mouth and take a breath before acting, how might you respond? These constructive responses are the beginning of your game plan. The behaviors in column 2 are going to happen, and they shouldn't surprise you. So spend some time preparing yourself.

Your students have already learned your triggers and understand your expectations, whether or not you've shared them explicitly. Your next step is to learn what triggers your *students* and figure out what you can do to set the tone for a regulated environment. Taking control of your responses to the absurd, the obnoxious, the disruptive, and the erratic events of your classroom goes a long way toward that goal.

Wrapping It Up

The exercise Pete shared reveals what I refer to as the "square peg, round hole" notion. We are given a large number of students to manage, and we do best when they act in ways that meet our needs. Face it: if you had a classroom of column 1 students, you would be a happy camper, right? Let's call that first list of desirable characteristics the "round holes." Unfortunately, classes like that don't grow on trees. Most of us get at least a few students who possess the attributes in column 2. I refer to these characteristics as our "square pegs." We often put a tremendous amount of effort into trying to make our square pegs fit into the round holes. We try and try to force those column 2 students to exhibit desirable behaviors, but, inevitably, the two will never fit.

What if we gave up the notion of the round hole and instead made room for a group of amoebas? Many of our students are just that: little amoebas trying to figure out what shape they want to become. Those growing up with adversity and trauma have not had permission to even explore that possibility. If we predefine students' shapes based on what works for us, we may be inadvertently adding to the effects of the trauma. We may be yet another person who is disrupting students' ability to define themselves. Although as adults, like children, we benefit from predictable environments, and our ability to self-regulate is crucial, we must find a way to balance it with the needs of our students. One cannot trump the other.

For some of you, I may have just caused a great deal of anxiety. It is difficult not to equate making that shift with losing control. But in reality, by making those adjustments and preparing rational responses for every scenario you might imagine, you most likely will end up having a *greater* sense of control. You will have granted those students permission to develop in a way that works for *them*, which will in turn better enable them to cultivate their self-regulation skills.

Reflective Questions

1.   Have you ever truly noticed your own breathing? When you actually focus on it, how is your breathing affected?

2.   What inner-peace activities do you do, if any? Yoga? Meditation? Deep breathing? Research a couple of these self-care methods and try them out to see if they might help you connect with yourself.

3.   Would any of these activities help your students? How so? Try at least one with your students, take notes on the results, and refine as necessary.

4.   Keep an ear out for the next time someone asks you, "Are you OK?" It might be a sign that you've drifted away from your baseline energy level. Can you sense it? Ask a trusted friend or colleague to describe how you're perceived when you're not at your baseline.

5.   Have you ever said something and immediately regretted it? Think about a particular time it happened. What was the trigger? What do you wish you had said or done instead?

6.   Try the "square peg, round hole" exercise. What do you notice about the behaviors that trigger you? Have you been aware of these behaviors before?

7.   After reading this chapter, is there anything you want to do differently to ensure you show positive responses to the student behaviors that frustrate you? Write a goal, create a time line, and share your progress with a trusted friend or colleague. Remember to celebrate when you've made some headway toward your goal!

6

It's Not About You

Incredible change happens in your life when you decide to
take control of what you do have power over instead of
craving control over what you don't.

—Steve Maraboli, *Life, the Truth, and Being Free*

. . . .

We work in a demanding, complicated field. The youngsters we work
with, whether in school, counseling, or clinical practice, are often
struggling with demons that we are unaware of or cannot comprehend.
It's important for us as caregivers and members of a service-oriented
profession to keep our focus on those whom we are serving, not on
ourselves.

This is easier said than done. After all, our work isn't just our voca-
tion; it's our livelihood. Our success is often evaluated by the success of
our students, so we have a vested interest in their outcomes and progress. However, it is vital for us to provide ethical and evidence-based
services that are oriented to our students' best interests. Everything we
say to and do with our students and families must be done solely for
their benefit, not our own. It's never about us. I repeat: it's not about
you.

Staying Focused

I have developed a set of three questions that I use regularly to help me stay focused on those I work with. These questions are

- What is my role?
- Who am I working for?
- What is about to drive my behavior?

Taking time to reflect on the answers to these questions helps us ensure that what we are doing is for students' benefit. Often, our need to get something accomplished, to say what we want to say, or to know a certain piece of information doesn't correspond to the student's need to do, hear, or share. Our need to tell isn't necessarily their need to listen, and our need to be understood shouldn't trump our need to *understand*. We must find out what students are asking for, help them make sense of that need, and teach them to express it in a productive way. The more aware we are of what drives our behavior, the more likely we are to make a choice that is in the best interest of the student.

In education, we strive to empower students to make positive choices for themselves and to work to their highest potential. Our overarching goal is to develop competent, capable adults who can contribute to society. However, that mission sometimes gets lost in the shuffle of our impatience, our protective nature, our fear, or our insistence that students do it *our* way. When these factors interfere, we end up taking away students' power to do, learn, and grow for themselves. How many times have you seen parents completing their child's science project? You get the idea. It happens more often than we care to admit.

Don't Sew Their Pillows

I use several analogies to illustrate how we can either empower or disempower students. One of them casts educators as lifeguards and students as swimmers. Often, students are barely keeping afloat amid the waves rocking their lives. They look to us to save them from such rough waters. But lifeguards aren't trained to dive into the deep end, swim up to the frantic, flailing victims, and save them; when they do that, they drown, too. How many times have you found yourself being pulled under by a student and drowning right alongside him or her? We must instead extend the victim a lifeline that says, "I have faith in your ability to swim." Identify the methods and strategies that communicate to students that you have faith in their ability to learn, grow, endure, and succeed. I know this seems like an overwhelming task. How do you find the right fit for students? How do you know a strategy will work? The good news is that this is not just on us, the adults. Students need to be active participants in relaying what is and isn't helpful. The more we find ways to partner with them around this, the better. We can empower them to learn healthy ways to maneuver through the troubled waters themselves.

Another way to look at this is to resolve not to "sew their pillows." So often, the students we work with have learned to get others to do for them, instead of learning to do for themselves. As a parent, I can relate to this reality. When I am busy, stressed, overwhelmed, and tired, it's easier just to do my kids' chores and provide immediate answers to their homework questions, skipping over the tedium of guiding them in the process of learning to do it for themselves. I'm guilty of having sewn my kids' pillows.

When our students wave their torn pillows in our faces, showing us the fraying seams with the stuffing hanging out, it is hard for us to ignore. Much of the damage they show us stems from experiences we know they should never have had. It is difficult to stay within our role when we feel such empathy. (And, let's face it, students seem to know just how to access our soft spots.) Sometimes, our immediate need to make it better overrides our long-term goal of empowering students to problem-solve on their own. We've got to do our best to stick to this long-term goal, though, and help students build up the resolve and grit that enable them to sew their own pillows. When we sew for them, we send two powerful, devastating messages: *You are incapable of doing this on your own* and *If you wait long enough and create enough of a fuss, someone will eventually do it for you.* Neither of these messages is healthy or positive, and neither aligns with the greater purpose of our profession.

Connect with the Right Before Redirecting with the Left

In times of crisis and conflict, effective communication is vital. We need to identify ways to communicate openly, honestly, and productively with our students, families, and clients. Healthy communication is a difficult enough course to navigate with just our own defenses and triggers. Add in our students' experiences of trauma, trust issues, and past letdowns, and the challenge is magnified significantly.

I am going to introduce you to a powerful series of six communication steps to begin using with your students and loved ones. I use these often in the couples therapy work that I do, and I swear by them in my interventions in the classroom setting with educators, administrators, students, and families. The steps are as follows:

1. Listen.
2. Reassure.
3. Validate.
4. Respond.
5. Repair.
6. Resolve.

Generally, we are experts at steps 1, 4, and 6. Unfortunately, we often skip steps 2, 3, and 5, which are essential to effective regulation and long-term relationship. Here's how our process typically works: we start with step 1, listening to someone express a concern. But instead of truly focusing on what is being said, we immediately begin to formulate our defense. We jump to step 4, which becomes our opportunity to share our defense. Then, if we're lucky, we skip to step 6 in the hope that we can prevent this situation from happening again. Sadly, we often miss the motive and the true meaning of the original message. By using communication shortcuts, we just set ourselves up to encounter the same problem further down the line.

Here's how to proceed through the steps effectively. First, **listen** deeply to the message being sent by your communication partner. Then pause for a moment to enact steps 2 and 3: **reassure** the person that his or her perspective is important, and **validate** his or her emotional state. Validating doesn't mean condoning or accepting responsibility for how the other is feeling; it merely means that we hear and acknowledge that this is his or her truth and experience. These two steps typically present the greatest challenge for most people, but they aren't time-consuming, and they set the stage for establishing a true connection that promises a healthy resolution. Building this emotional connection is a prerequisite for conducting a rational, robust conversation and for building and sustaining a meaningful relationship. As I like to put it, we must connect with the *right* (i.e., the emotional part of the brain) before we can redirect with the *left* (i.e., the logical part of the brain).

Validating another's perspective requires us to be in our upstairs brain, which can be challenging when we're feeling attacked or vulnerable. Our best bet is to try to usher our companion into his or her upstairs brain as well. When we believe that we are being heard and understood, we are far more inclined to engage in a healthy conversation that leads to a positive resolution. We *all* need to be validated and reassured in some way—to be able to process our feelings of stress and frustration and know that others understand what we are experiencing.

After steps 2 and 3, you have the opportunity to **respond** (step 4) and engage in a **repair** (step 5). A response is an explanation, not a defending statement, about what actually occurred through your lens. If you have successfully validated and reassured the person you are communicating with, the response becomes the explanation for the behavior versus the justification for your action. If done correctly, this can offer insight into the situation and offer an alternative perspective on the intent behind the action.

A repair includes a heartfelt apology for whatever role you may have played in the miscommunication or strife. Even if you don't believe you were in the wrong, an earnest apology can go a long way in building trust. It doesn't necessarily mean you're accepting responsibility for what took place, just that you can recognize the other person's experience and are sorry things turned out the way they did. And when you *do* have some responsibility for the situation, acknowledging your part in it honestly and humbly can lead to great strides in building trust and relationship. The goal of repair is to attempt to heal the rupture in the relationship and to begin identifying alternative ways of managing to avoid a similar disruption in the future.

Repair is one of the biggest steps we miss in education. So often, we mistake a student's return to regulation as a form of repair. But getting a student to a place of being able to return to the classroom does not constitute repair; it just means that the student may now be primed to reflect on what happened so that repair can actually take place. In addition, many of our students and staff have never had healthy repair modeled for them, so the concept is foreign. Many families engage in the pattern of rupture-separate-return, in which a disruption, argument, or hurtful exchange occurs; the parties involved separate from each other; and, after time passes, they return and act as though nothing happened. Opting not to address what occurred leaves a void of understanding and a lingering fear that the upset may happen again. We have a huge responsibility to model what healthy repair looks like and to incorporate structures into our discipline and corrective policies that enable this step to take place.

After a successful repair, the **resolution** (step 6) can truly happen. Resolution means coming to terms with what happened and collaborating to find alternative ways of acting to prevent future disruptions of the same type. This process involves addressing the questions, *How do we keep this from happening again? What can we do differently to ensure that this will not happen again? Are there other people we need to involve so that they, too, can know how we hope to act differently?*

If you have completed steps 1–5, you have also given yourself the gift of reflection: an opportunity to look back on what happened and gain insight on what led to this outcome as well as to wonder what you might do differently in the future. So many of us repeatedly engage in the same dance with our students and then wonder why things aren't getting better. When you find this happening to you, ask yourself if you have truly engaged in the six-step communication process and given all parties the chance to reflect and explore alternative solutions. How can you partner with this student, colleague, or parent in a different way to leave room for a more positive and productive outcome?

The Angry Mother

Let's apply this communication process to a scenario many of us have had the misfortune to experience: an encounter with an angry parent. Johnny's mom is coming in *hot*. She is ready to take you on, and she is not afraid to show it. (If this is already triggering you and sending you to your downstairs brain, remember: when in doubt, shut your mouth and take a breath.) She barges into your classroom after school and accuses you of calling her kid "stupid" and playing favorites with the other students. She claims that Johnny has no chance of success because you have it in for him—and he knows it.

At this point, most of us would be lining up our defenses and coming up with a rational response that shuts down these accusations. Some of us would also be formulating a way to convince her that her child truly is a pain. We are ready to defend ourselves and put this woman in her place.

But now I want you to pause and try something different: just reflect on what is happening in front of you. Do you think this parent is in her downstairs brain? Of course she is! Some of the 1st graders I work with would tell you that she is "in her basement"! Now ask yourself how well this conversation will go if she remains in that part of her brain. Not well, right? No one can engage in healthy discussion without being in the rational part of the brain. So instead of reacting immediately, think for a moment and try to decipher what is *really* being said. Clearly, this mother is angry and needs you to know how she and her son are feeling. The first step is to try to connect with the *right* so we can have more options for redirecting with the *left*. Here's a response that reflects this process:

> I am so glad that you came to see me. Thank you for bringing this to my attention. Not all parents I work with have the courage to talk to a teacher about their concerns for their child. It is obvious to me how much you care about Johnny and his experience at this school. I can tell that you are really angry and upset with me right now. I completely understand why you might be. If I thought my son's teacher hated him and called him stupid, I would be pretty ticked off as well. Let's talk more about how you and Johnny came to feel this way.

While you're engaging in steps 2 and 3, what do you think is happening for this mom? Do you think you are setting the table to have a meaningful conversation about her son?

You continue with your response:

> I want you to know that I do enjoy having Johnny in class, and I feel terrible that you and he think otherwise. If there is anything I have said or done that led you and Johnny to think that I do not like him, I am truly sorry, and I would be more than happy to apologize to Johnny as well. It is never my intention to lead a student to believe that I do not like him or her.

Step 5 is a good time to insert a couple of heartfelt compliments:

> The truth is, I think Johnny is great. I really enjoy having him in class, and I am especially grateful when he offers to help with organizing or handing out materials. He does seem to do better work when he sits apart from the other students. This isn't intended to make him feel left out or different; it's just that he's more focused and performs better on his assignments when I give him the opportunity to work independently, without distraction. I am sorry if today he felt like I was calling him stupid. That was certainly not the case, and if he thought that was what I meant, I will apologize to him immediately.

Finally, you can look forward with step 6:

> Let's put a plan in place that addresses the concerns we talked about today. I really want Johnny to be successful in my class, and I would value your help in achieving that. What do you think may help with this situation? Here are some thoughts I am having.... Let's also invite Johnny to offer his input on what he thinks may help. Once we decide on and implement a solution, we can meet again in a couple of weeks to touch base and see how things are going. I will work on giving Johnny some more praise and encouragement, and I would appreciate it if you could help him remember to ask me—by raising his hand and waiting for me to come to him—if he needs help understanding our classwork. Does that sound like a good start?

This conversation, which appeared doomed from the start, actually seems to be headed toward a positive and mutually beneficial resolution. How would this conversation be different if you had attended only to steps 1, 4, and 6? Can you picture the result of two downstairs brains colliding? It is much more effective to direct the conversation through all six steps of the communication process.

The more we learn to take ourselves out of the equation and focus on the student, his or her family, and the issue at hand, the more likely it is that we will be successful in our interactions.

PETE'S PRACTICE

I had the pleasure of working alongside an assistant principal, Mrs. Romey, who taught me a ton about the use of the "It's not about you" approach. I often marveled at the way she interacted with angry students, fired-up parents, and irritated teachers in the heat of the moment. She never took any of it personally.

A chunk of Mrs. Romey's responsibility involved student discipline. As a middle school assistant principal, she had her fair share of office referrals to work through. One particular situation caught my attention, when an 8th grade student was sent to the office for creating a scene and refusing to follow the teacher's directions.

By the time the young man, Adam, made it to the office, he had worked himself up into quite a lather. Mrs. Romey welcomed him and asked him to share his side of the story. Adam ranted about his teacher, his classmates, and the ridiculous rules that made it impossible for him to stay motivated. Calmly, Mrs. Romey said, "I'm sorry to hear that. Which rules, in particular, are you frustrated with?"

Adam responded with a tirade that would make most sailors blush. After spewing f-bombs and comments about Mrs. Romey's choice in career, body parts, and mother's attire, he finished with "You don't fricking care anyway, bitch!"

Mrs. Romey remained as composed as ever, replying, "I do care, and I want to hear your concerns so we can make this a better learning experience for you. I can tell that you feel passionately about your education and your future, and you're upset that it's being interrupted like this. Let's see if we can work together to figure out where this went wrong so it doesn't happen again."

Disarmed, Adam looked up at Mrs. Romey. "Why don't you ever yell at me?" he asked. Unfazed, Mrs. Romey replied, "Now, why would I yell at a smart, capable young man who's angry about something? Where would that get us?" Adam squinted his eyes for a moment and then sat silently. He was ready to proceed with a conversation.

As she so often did, Mrs. Romey had turned a potentially volatile situation—one in which she could easily have taken up Adam's gauntlet and punished him with out-of-school suspension—into a brainstorming session in which Adam took some ownership of his own actions and created a plan for improving his behaviors. Mrs. Romey also orchestrated a repair-focused reentry meeting with Adam's teacher prior to the next day's class. It was yet another lesson for me that "It's not about you."

Wrapping It Up

In this chapter, I have suggested that we maintain our focus on the students we serve. In theory, this seems like a grand idea that should be easy to implement. However, I'm a realist. I know it isn't easy, especially when we're bombarded with messaging telling us that "It starts with you." We're constantly worried about what people will say about us and how we're perceived. I've often asked myself, *Am I effective? Is my work good enough? Have I met my goals? What else do I need to do? Where do I go from here?*

In my discussion of the six-step communication process, I mentioned that we often feel the need to defend our position and our actions. The reality is you have nothing to defend. You are doing the best you can with what you have in the moment. Keep in mind, too, that your communication partner is also doing the best he or she can. If you can remember that, you will learn not to personalize charged situations as much and move your practice in a healthier direction.

Reflective Questions

1. What is your role?
2. Who are you working for?
3. What is about to drive your behavior?
4. When you consider the three questions above, do you have a consistent basis for answering them? How do your responses demonstrate whether your focus is on yourself or your students?
5. Think of a time when you sewed somebody else's pillows. What was the situation? Why did you intervene? What need were you addressing? How might you have handled it differently, if you had paused and thought about it first?
6. When was the last time you were in a heated, emotional argument? Did you attempt steps 2, 3, and 5 in the six-step communication process? Why or why not? If you did use them, what was the outcome? If you didn't, do you think the outcome would have been different if you had used them? Why or why not?
7. What is your response to my claim that "you are doing the best you can with what you have in the moment"? Do you agree? Disagree? Why? Does your answer change when you think about the person with whom you are having the disagreement? Why or why not?

PART III

Relationship

Love does not measure, it just gives.

—Mother Teresa

• • • • • • • • • • • • • • • •

The work we do is never done in isolation. By design, schools are places where humans interact. Teachers, students, parents, administrators, counselors, and others are organized in such a fashion to support one another in reaching our mutual goals. We are interdependent. To say it would be a challenge to accomplish our work individually is an understatement: it would be an outright impossibility.

The relationships we forge and maintain with others are essential to our collective and individual success. As the old saying goes, "It takes a village to raise a child." What, then, does it take to raise an entire community of children? We must all work together, embracing one another's strengths, weaknesses, tendencies, idiosyncrasies, and personalities to move forward, learning and growing in partnership and collaboration.

Relationships are not easy. They are complex, dynamic, and somewhat irrational bonds between people that sometimes seem to fluctuate more than the weather. Just managing "normal" relationships with our friends, coworkers, and family can be challenging. When we bring trauma-affected students into the equation, the delicate nature of relationships stands out even more clearly.

In Chapter 7, I ask you to define—and then to redefine—your understanding of the term *relationship*. You may be surprised by the assumptions you bring to the table, especially when considering how relationships affect your professional role. For now, here's a preliminary definition from our friends from *Winnie-the-Pooh* (Milne, 1928):

> Piglet sidled up to Pooh from behind. "Pooh!" he whispered.
> "Yes, Piglet?"
> "Nothing," said Piglet, taking Pooh's paw. "I just wanted to be sure of you."

This excerpt offers a nice glimpse into what constitutes a relationship. In my practice and trainings, I advocate for the cultivation of positive relationships as the first step in problem solving, decision making, or any course of action. Taking this step leads us to listen more, to understand others' perspectives, and to develop empathy. I believe these are incredibly valuable strategies for engaging in work of any kind with another human being.

In the following four chapters, I share strategies that are rooted in the belief that relationships matter. Relationships require an investment of time, energy, and spirit, and the payoff isn't for you alone; remember, it's not about you but about the students you serve. However, the benefits tend to multiply in the context of a strong, true relationship—helping us all.

7

No One Said Relationship Is Easy

These children aren't seeking attention (even though they will settle for it). They are looking for a safe and trustworthy relationship (connection). (Marvin et al., 2002)

. . . .

No one said relationship is easy. In fact, creating and sustaining a relationship with someone is one of the hardest things we can do. It takes effort, patience, and, most important, *grace*—a word I discuss in depth in Chapter 14.

All too often, I hear that too much is asked of us as professionals. Guess what? It's true! But we need to find a way to cultivate strong, meaningful connections with our students anyway. For elementary classroom teachers, that means building and nurturing about 30 relationships over the course of a school year; for administrators, coun-selors, and teachers in secondary schools, that number climbs into the hundreds or even the thousands—with shorter windows in which to interact with each student. That doesn't even account for the dozens (or hundreds) of families we consistently communicate with. Building this many relationships may seem like an unrealistic expectation, but it's actually quite possible. It just may require us to tweak our definition of *relationship* and how that definition is manifested in our roles.

Let's begin by examining the term *relationship*. What does this word mean to you? What does it mean for you to have a relationship with someone else? What does that look like?

 Write down the words and phrases that define the term *rela-tionship* for you. If it helps, provide a couple of examples and describe those specific relationships.

We tend to place a lot of unnecessary pressure on ourselves to cre-ate intense, enduring relationships. Many of us in the field harbor the belief that we must be everything to every student we work with, and that is a daunting proposition indeed.

Powerful Relationships

Emotional, lasting relationships do occur in our work. There are stu-dents who enter our lives and leave an eternal imprint on our hearts. These special relationships embody our personal definition of *relation-ship*. For these students, we went the extra mile. We gave our time and energy to ensure their success and well-being. We truly, deeply cared about them; in fact, we *still* care about them, no matter how long ago they touched our hearts. We wonder how they are doing, where they are, whom they are with, whether they are safe or not, how happy they are, and what their lives are like. The longer we're in this business, the more lives we touch, and the more likely it is that our former students are now adults with children of their own, living lives unknown to us.

Take a moment to honor one of these special relationships. Allow yourself to smile at a memory or even shed a tear to reflect the emotion you feel for this person. Give yourself permission to honor a relationship that had meaning to you. These are the moments that keep us working, and these are the people who inspire us to continue.

I have learned over the years that we are all drawn to certain characteristics, interests, or mannerisms in others. The fact that we find these attributes more appealing than others facilitates the relationship-building process. Is this true of our work with students? Are we more likely to be drawn to the stories that have greater meaning to us? Are we more apt to break down barriers and "go to bat" for those with whom we connect more easily? Absolutely. This is human nature, and we must acknowledge that reality. It doesn't mean that we don't try hard with all of our students; rather, it explains why some relationships are stronger and develop more quickly than others do.

Think back to the relationship you reflected on two paragraphs ago. What was special about this individual? How was your relationship with this student different from those with other students? What about his or her story moved you or inspired you to go beyond the call of duty? As you explore these factors, embrace the reality that every relationship is unique. This is a healthy way to pay attention to ourselves and to learn what we're drawn to. If we are more sensitive to a specific situation, need, or trait, gaining an awareness of this will help us better understand our capacity for relationship with the students we work with. All too often, we ignore our own sensitivities and inclinations and just "push through," mechanically trying to form relationships because we know how important they are for our students, particularly those affected by trauma. Connecting to ourselves, however, is a crucial step in offering transparency and congruence to our personal mission and our true selves, which help us build authentic, enduring relationships. When we are real with ourselves, we give our students permission to be real with themselves—and we can form real relationships together.

Safe Enough, Healthy Enough

As wonderful as those deep, enduring relationships are, they aren't the norm. Attempting to build dozens, hundreds, or even thousands of such relationships is not a realistic expectation for any of us. It *is* possible, however, for each of us to be *safe enough* and *healthy enough* for every person in our lives, thereby establishing an environment ripe for strong, lasting relationships.

How might we begin to alter our definition of *relationship* to include everyone we work with, not just the special few with whom we share a special bond? We can be creative in adapting our relationships with students so that they all feel some connection with us. The first step is to think of ourselves as being "safe enough" and "healthy enough" for students—because for the most part, that is all our kids really need from us.

If we can provide consistency, positivity, and integrity in all our interactions with our students, we'll establish a relationship that is safe enough for them. And if we initiate a repair whenever necessary, earnestly working to model and engage in appropriate interpersonal behaviors, we can cultivate an environment that is healthy enough for them. If they know we will be relentless in our support of their endeavors, forgive them the errors they make along the way, and maintain our determination that they will live up to their potential and our expectations, then the relationships will follow. Nothing more than that is required.

Sonja's Story

Several years ago, I worked with a high school student in my private practice. Sonja had worked up the courage to ask her mom if she could see a counselor, since her graduation was approaching and she wanted strategies to manage her anxiety. As I got to know Sonja, I learned that she had a GPA close to 4.0 and a solid friend base—along with an extensive history of trauma. Her ACE score was 7, including a history of sexual and physical abuse, witnessing of domestic violence, drug and alcohol abuse in the home, multiple moves, abandonment by a primary caregiver, and neglect. Her resilience and the success she had achieved despite her numerous not-OK experiences were amazing to me.

One of the first things I address with clients is safety. When I asked Sonja to think about who was safe for her when she was growing up, she looked at me like I had three heads. She had never thought about people in terms of the safety they offered, let alone given herself permission to reflect on her childhood experiences of safe people. Because the majority of her abuse had occurred during her younger years, and her family had never stayed in one place for long, she had had little opportunity to build any kind of relationship with another person. She was so overwhelmed by this question that she asked me if she could think about it and answer it at our next session.

At the next session, she said that after a great deal of thinking, she had finally come up with an answer. She described a time when she was about 7 or 8, when she and her mom were living with one of her mom's boyfriends in a trailer park. Her mom was working several jobs to pay the bills, so Sonja was often left alone with this boyfriend. Being abusive, he was anything but safe for her; in fact, being alone with him terrorized her. She then described an elderly woman who lived next door to them. Every afternoon at 3:00, this woman would sit out on her porch. Eventually, Sonja learned that she was welcome to join this neighbor, and sitting together on the porch, eating a cookie or ice cream, became a regular ritual for them.

Some days, however, it was not safe for Sonja to leave the trailer. If the boyfriend happened to be in the living room, he could see Sonja as she walked out the front door, and she had learned to stay off his radar in the hope that he would forget she was there. When it was too risky to expose herself, Sonja would hide quietly in her bedroom. She began leaving a sign in her bedroom window for the neighbor that read, "Can't come out today."

The elderly woman, who had come to expect Sonja at 3:00, worried about her on the days she did not show and one day walked over to Sonja's trailer. When she spotted the sign, she pulled over a lawn chair and sat underneath Sonja's window for the usual afternoon period. She did this every time Sonja stayed home. Sonja learned that no matter what, she could count on this woman to be there for her every day at 3:00.

As Sonja told me this story, she became tearful and said, "You know the funny thing about this whole story? We never even bothered to learn each other's names. But she was my safe person, and I credit her for where I am today."

Being Available

Sonja's elderly neighbor was safe enough and healthy enough to build a bond with Sonja, just by being there every day. This is such a powerful story for many reasons: it's a great example of how we can rethink ways to be available to our students, it models a safe and healthy relationship, it shows how relationships can simultaneously be simple yet deep, and it conjures some powerful emotions. This elderly woman will never know how much of a difference she made to Sonja. She will never know that the simple act of being there for someone every day at 3:00 made all the difference in the world to a child who was suffering. How can we begin to think of ourselves as someone who is always there, every day, at 3:00? Sometimes that kind of predictability and consistency is all a student needs to build resiliency and learn a different way of being.

Think of the students you work with who are struggling for various reasons. Consider the ways you can be available to them "every day at 3:00." What might that look like? The thoughts you record are the beginning of your revised definition of the term *relationship*.

Now review what you just wrote. Compare your thoughts with your original definition of *relationship*. Does the prospect of building relationships start to feel more "doable" for *all* the students and families you interact with?

We can take some simple steps to create an environment that is safe enough and healthy enough for our students. It starts with how we set the table: the way we communicate, attune to students' moods and emotions, hold them accountable to our expectations, provide consistency, offer second chances, and model the characteristics of healthy relationships. What do you do in your daily practice to set the table for students?

PETE'S PRACTICE

Betsy, a 7th and 8th grade special education teacher, seemed to have a strong personal relationship with every student on her caseload, in her classes, and in the hallway. I marveled at the number of students who exchanged hellos and smiles with Betsy in any setting on campus, and I wondered how she managed this.

It wasn't long before the simple answer came to me. I was walking through the hallways of our middle school during passing period, and as the students reached their destinations, I stopped outside Betsy's classroom door. There she was, standing in the doorway, welcoming every student who entered with a pleasant smile and a cheerful greeting like "Good afternoon, I'm glad to see you today."

Every student matched the eye contact and the handshake, providing some sort of response to Betsy before entering the room. "This is our little ritual," Betsy explained to me. "I know that during the course of the class period, I may not be able to give each student my undivided attention, so I want to make sure that we start on the right foot and that I let them know I care about each and every one of them." It wasn't a major time commitment—the greeting took less than seven seconds per student—but it was a massive investment in relationships that paid off in classroom management, engagement, and achievement.

Wrapping It Up

James Comer (1995) once said, "No significant learning occurs without a significant relationship." Adding to that, generations of educators have heard some variation on the saying "Students don't care to learn until we learn to care." The power of relationship is clear and compelling, and we know we must tend to the many relationships we have built with colleagues, families, and, of course, our students. For students who have experienced trauma, forging strong relationships is not simple. Because the source of many students' trauma is another human being, distrust and a hesitancy to bond with others are common. Rather than forcing the issue and attempting to create a connection that will "save" a particular student, it's more effective for us to concentrate on simply being safe enough and healthy enough for all the students who enter our domain. We may not see the results immediately, and we may not have that emotional, inseparable bond with every young person who needs it, but with consistency and faith, we can know that our effect will be felt far beyond our time together in the classroom.

Reflective Questions

1. Ask a colleague, a spouse, or a trusted friend to define *relationship*. Share your definitions and discuss what they mean to you. What do they have in common? What distinguishes them?

2. Did your definition of *relationship* change as you read this chapter? How so?

3. How might your revised definition of *relationship* allow you to reduce the pressure you put on yourself to be "everything to everyone" in your professional responsibilities?

4. Spend some time brainstorming ways to be "safe enough" for all your students. What might you have to do to remain cognizant of these strategies during your work?

5. Compile a list of ways that you can be "healthy enough" for all your students. Are these strategies manageable enough for you to use on a regular basis?

6. What was your emotional response to Sonja's story? Do you have students who have similar stories? How might you focus on being there for them "at 3:00" every day, even if you don't know what their trauma histories are?

7. What rituals have you developed to "set the table" with your students, your teams, your classes, and your daily routines? What might your students say about these?

8

The Power of Relationship

You see, you closed your eyes. That was the difference.
Sometimes you cannot believe what you see, you have to
believe what you feel. And, if you are ever going to have
other people trust you, you must feel that you can trust
them, too—even when you're in the dark. Even when you
are falling.

—Mitch Albom, *Tuesdays with Morrie*

. . . .

Trust is a fundamental part of a healthy relationship. A healthy relationship, in turn, is an instrumental aspect of feeling safe—and a sense of safety enables students who have experienced trauma to stay regulated and access the healthy parts of their brain. One of the most powerful and rewarding ways we can help our students flourish is to provide the safety of a trusting, healthy relationship.

You can become that safe place for students, that person they can rely on for support and empowerment. Whether you work with students every day or just a short time each week, the consistency of your presence and influence provides the foundation for building a safe and sustainable relationship with every student in your care.

Safety First

In 2007, ASCD launched its Whole Child Initiative, which promotes children's long-term development and success rather than narrowly defined academic achievement. The whole child approach (see http://www.wholechildeducation.org/about) aims at ensuring that every student is healthy, safe, engaged, supported, and challenged. The second tenet—safety—states, "Each student learns in an environment that is physically and emotionally safe for students and adults." According to *Educating the Whole Child* (Brown, 2008), here are some factors that contribute to that safety:

- The school grounds and building are safe and secure.
- School staff clearly articulate and implement behavioral expectations and procedures.
- Family members are welcomed as partners in their children's education and can communicate directly with the school and staff members.
- School staff model prosocial behaviors, including kindness and respect for others.

I would like to add the following factors that contribute to a safe classroom environment:

- *Assigned seating*. Assigned seats communicate to students that they are supposed to be there and they have a place where they belong.
- *Check-in and check-out*. School staff members show they care by doing a "temperature check" each morning and afternoon to see how each student is doing.
- *Posting of pictures*. Photos of students throughout the classroom and school send a message of family and belonging.

- *Notes or calls home.* When teachers call or send notes home, they're saying, "I care about your well-being and your success. You are important to me, and I am here for you."
- *Rituals.* Implementing regular rituals and routines—for example, daily greetings or announcements—helps students know what to expect from their teachers and their day.

Balancing the Two Pieces: Availability and Accountability

When students are struggling and acting outside the conditions we have set for learning success, it throws us off. Often, our own need for structure and predictability is thrown into orbit when we are faced with a student who has shut down and refuses to learn or is outright defiant. As pressures on educators continue to mount, I'm noticing a shift toward the belief that discipline is the answer to "fixing these broken kids": we need to come down harder and hold such a black-and-white expectation that all students will eventually fall in line. Sadly, this is not the answer. Forced compliance does not teach accountability, and severe consequences and removal from the classroom do not induce learning; they actually set kids up to fail.

Don't get me wrong: I am all for accountability and personal responsibility. I just think students need some alternative options to manage their intense emotions and reactions. Usually when they misbehave, they are only showing us what they know. They don't necessarily like acting out any more than we like it; most times, in fact, they are terrified of having that much power. The problem is that we have often inadvertently expressed to these students that we cannot handle their intensity—that we are overwhelmed by their needs and are at a complete loss as to how to respond.

Students need to be held accountable for respecting themselves and others, but not by being beaten into submission. Most students who are acting out have been beaten down enough. Instead, we need to show them a window into a different way of managing how they handle their emotions.

Experiencing trauma does not excuse unsafe or harmful behavior, nor should it support distraction from learning. Yet it is scary for students to see that things could be different. Children early on identify ways of managing their stress, healthy or not, and those coping methods become patterns of behavior. Learning and practicing a different way of coping, although better, is not easy or comfortable. It is terrifying for them to ponder what life could be like without abuse or stress, however inconceivable that may seem to some of us. Envisioning alternatives means seeing their caregiver in a new light, which takes an abundance of courage. I was working with a 3rd grader whose answer to anything unsettling was to punch or throw things. As a result, he spent many an afternoon in the principal's office or in detention. When I asked him what his behavior was about, he replied, "This is how we roll in my family. If you want something done or if something makes you mad, you hit to get your way." I asked him, "How's that working for you?" He responded with a smile, "Not so great." Still, I acknowledged that learning to do things differently from the way he was taught would be hard. Challenging ourselves to find new, healthy ways of coping takes time, patience, and the support of others.

Helping students gain awareness of their stress response and teaching them positive ways to respond to stress are key steps that help them deal with all kinds of challenges. As adults, we are responsible both for providing safety and for maintaining expectations. Balancing these two demands is one of the biggest challenges educators grapple with. I often see one of the two following scenarios in schools:

• Teachers are so trauma-aware and sensitive to students' situations that they provide only the empathy and availability piece. They are strictly relational and struggle with holding students accountable for the way they manage their intensity.

- Teachers are so focused on student accountability that they ignore the relational piece. They are intent on showing students that regardless of their adverse experiences, they are expected to meet a strict standard of behavior and self-management.

Neither of these systems works. In your own way, you must find a balance. Don't worry about being perfect. Kent Hoffman, one of my mentors within the Circle of Security project (http://circleofsecurity .net), always reminded me that I only have to get it right 3 out of 10 times to make a child feel secure (being sure to repair the other 7 times).

I have modeled countless interventions for teachers whose students have "flipped their lids" and are truly in their downstairs brain. Successful interventions balance the two pieces of accountability and availability. First, validating students' feelings and reassuring them that they are safe and will get through this moment form a connection that is crucial to getting a student back to a regulated state. Once students are regulated (which may require a few laps around the hallways or several minutes of sitting in silence), we can help them see the big picture of what happened versus just their experience of what happened. From there, we can start to explore what self-respect and respect of others could have looked like, connect students to the intensity they felt in their bodies that led to the lid flip, explore alternative ways of managing that intensity, and help them see that they do have some control in their lives.

Anthony's Story

Several years ago, I was working at an elementary school where I had begun to bond with a kindergartner named Anthony. Based on his behaviors and his frequent lid flips, I suspected that Anthony, who was in foster care, was being abused. As we slowly connected, he began to take more risks with me. He would look for me to enter the classroom and smile when he saw me, and eventually he invited me to read with him. Once, as we looked at a picture of a mom hugging her daughter, he mentioned that he never got hugged like that. This was as personal as he got. Sometimes he would let me rub his back or hug his shoulder, but he wouldn't permit any more contact than that.

His teacher and I worked together to figure out what kind of repair might work with him after he flipped and how we could start to integrate accountability into his repertoire. I found myself getting frustrated with other staff members who described him in a negative light because they were so exhausted from his behaviors. I would take a breath and say, "It looks to me like he is asking for help. I wonder what life must be like for a 5-year-old who has never known what *safe* felt like. I can't imagine how difficult it must be to enter a new setting with such high expectations and have no knowledge of how to fulfill them." This seemed to help.

We all kept at it, and Anthony had good days and not-so-good days. One day, when we were out on the playground, I watched Anthony let out a genuine belly laugh. He had begun to experience how enjoyable it could be to play with other students. He was holding his own, and I could tell he was feeling great. As we all filed back into the building, one of the other students begged to hold my hand (as several thousand kindergartners do every day), which I of course agreed to. I noticed Anthony watching and gave him a smile, sending the nonverbal message that this was an OK thing to do. He then walked up to his teacher and slowly put his hand in hers. She took it without skipping a beat. To this day, I am not sure she was aware of the impact that this moment had. Something so natural and routine for her had begun to change the course of this child's experience. I watched Anthony stare at their hands with a kind of awe. Just before we got to the classroom, he turned back and smiled at me. The smile said, "This feels good and safe." It was as if in that moment, he got to experience what a healthy connection could feel like. Later that day, when I checked back in on him, his teacher said in wonder, "He is having an amazing day." I walked over to him, and he proudly showed me his star chart. He had earned two stars that day—the most he had ever earned.

Although I know life isn't simple enough that this standout day would fix Anthony's problems, I also know that our willingness to provide a safe place for him and our commitment to showing him something different from what his experience of relationship had taught him helped him build up the courage to explore a new way of being. He was able to start attempting to trust. He was able to form a connection with an adult that didn't involve abuse or consequence. It is these moments that give students hope and fresh insight into what their lives could be.

That Teacher

Take a moment and think of an education professional who had a positive effect on your life.

 Write down the name of a teacher who made a difference in your life:

What was it about this person that motivated you to learn, to come to school, to try your hardest? What was it about this educator that inspired you to do what you do today? What traits did you appreciate about this person? Write down some words or phrases that describe this person and his or her influence on you:

This person made a huge difference in your life, possibly unknowingly. His or her simple way of being may have been enough for you to want to do more. Perhaps this person was strict and found ways to challenge you to go beyond your comfort zone, or maybe he or she was gentle and kind and took the time to ask how you were doing. Maybe this person made a point to eat lunch with you or showed up to one of your events to cheer you on. Conjuring up these images and memories might be enough to inspire you to write this person a thank-you note or pick up the phone to convey your feelings. If so, go for it!

Although I had the privilege of having many wonderful teachers throughout my educational experience, my high school English teacher Dr. Birrer is the one who sticks out most in my memory. This is probably because I had her during a stressful period in my life, and I was raised in a time when it was truly *not* OK to acknowledge being not-OK and talk about the tough stuff. During my time in her class, she didn't do anything extraordinary; she was just dependable and consistent. Her enthusiasm about English literature was contagious, and for one hour each day, I could escape from whatever was stressful in my life. I knew I could count on her passion for the subject and her tenacity in teaching. I even wrote her a thank-you letter after I graduated from college, sharing that I was working the uneventful night shift at a residential facility. And do you know what? She wrote me back with a three-page list of classics to read during that shift. Dr. Birrer was an inspiration to me. To this day, I emulate her in my work teaching graduate students.

I know there are thousands of folks out there who make a difference for students. Pete and I come across so many teachers and education professionals in our work who connect with students in a positive way. I am sure many of you have come across those professionals who made it a point to have lunch with a struggling student, attended a sporting event because they knew a student wouldn't have a support system in the audience, took time out of their schedule to provide extra tutoring, or simply offered a safe space for kids.

PETE'S PRACTICE

The simple message of "Good morning!" is a powerful one for many of us, and it can help set the mood for the day. I love the many variations: "Top o' the mornin' to ya," "Buenos días, amigo!" and even a simple, cheerful "Hello!" The acknowledgment of life and the joy of being seen by someone provide a little ray of sunshine that establishes the tone for everything that follows.

Kristin often mentions that one of the reasons she wanted to collaborate with me was the fact that as a principal, I prioritized the cultivation of meaningful relationships. I made an effort to learn the names of all the students in my building as soon as school started. I wanted to know about them, as students and as young people. With this knowledge, I was able to harness what I call "the power of seven seconds" (Hall, 2011). Think of it this way: every morning, every student who enters the school has a story. It might be a story of hugs and breakfast and toothbrushing, or it might be a story of fitful sleep, an absentee parent, and a fight with a sibling. We don't know these stories, and we can't control what has already happened. But we *can* control our ability to say, "Good morning!" right off the bat.

The first seven seconds of our interaction with every student in our school should be brimming with enthusiasm, joy, compliments, or some sort of friendly banter. It doesn't take any longer than that to make someone's day, no matter how his or her day began. If we allocate those seven seconds wisely, saying, "Good morning, Jackie, thanks for bringing that sunshine in today. How's your new puppy?" instead of "Excuse me, you need to take your hat off inside, young lady," then we've taken a big step toward starting each youngster's day with a smile.

All it takes to do this is a little heart, a little dedication, and a little willingness to commit to establishing relationships. What follows is a mood enhancer for everyone involved.

Wrapping It Up

Relationship, by definition, is a two-way street. It requires two people's heartfelt effort. We can't expect our students to have faith and trust in us if we don't give them the same in return. Think about it: have you ever had a true relationship with someone who didn't trust you? Conversely, could you be honest and transparent with someone who wasn't honest and transparent with you? It doesn't work that way.

This doesn't mean that you stop being the adult and start acting like your students' best friend. It means that you have the same faith in them that you expect them to have in you. Above all, your relationships with students need to be authentic and sincere. Kids, particularly those who have experienced trauma, can see right through the façade of an insincere relationship.

Students who have been exposed to trauma have learned to cue off their environment. They have learned early on what is safe and what is not safe. They have learned from experience when it is OK to ask for a need to be met and when it is important to do for themselves. They take these same survival skills into the classroom with them. They are constantly reading their environment—and you—to determine their level of safety. It is up to us to reinforce that they are in fact safe and that they can trust their environment.

Reflective Questions

1. Review the Whole Child Initiative's list of ways to provide a safe environment for your students. How many of them do you employ? Which ones could you implement?

2. Go back to "that teacher." If you were to write a thank-you letter to that person, what would it say? What were the big lessons you learned from this great educator?

3.   Do you see any of that great teacher's characteristics in the way you teach? How so?

4.   Tomorrow, take note of how you greet each of your students. What are the first words each young person hears you say?

5.   Can you commit to investing seven seconds to make a student's day? Most likely, you know which students need that pep talk the most. Jot down some notes of what you will say to those students tomorrow.

6.   When was the last time you ruptured a relationship with another person? How did you handle it? Did you repair? Did the other person? Why or why not?

7.   How can you compel yourself to repair with another person when it's necessary? Would it help to write down some key words, so that you can remember the six steps of effective communication?

9

Names, Labels, and the Need for Control

I don't have enough letters next to my name to be able to work with that kid.

—Anonymous teacher

. . . .

I hear some variation on the words above often in my work with education professionals. Many teachers simply do not feel equipped to work with the students who have been assigned to their classrooms. I hear things like, "Students are different today," "It's not like it used to be," and "Kids these days are allowed to get away with a lot more than I ever was."

Why is this the dominant discourse? I'm guessing that every generation has lamented the seemingly incorrigible nature of the next generation. Guess who uttered these words: "Our youth now love luxury.

They have bad manners, contempt for authority; they show disrespect for their elders and love chatter in place of exercise; they no longer rise when elders enter the room; they contradict their parents, chatter before company, gobble up their food, and tyrannize their teachers." If you answered Socrates (quoted in Patty & Johnson, 1953, p. 277), complaining sometime around 400 B.C.E., you are correct.

This disapproval of youth and the accompanying befuddlement over how to deal with them are clearly not a new phenomenon, but they are real issues, and our teachers are crying out for help. Unfortunately, this leads to controversy over who should be allowed in a classroom, how much misbehavior should be tolerated, and if and when teachers and school officials should have the right to dismiss a student from a classroom or from school itself. This is unfortunate because it focuses too much on reactive consequence and discipline and not on proactive ways of changing the discourse and keeping students in school and helping them thrive—that is, this perspective is adult-centered and deficit-focused rather than student-centered and strength-focused. Fixating on problems may offer validation for how hard our jobs are, but it leaves us short of identifying all our students'—and our own—strengths.

Consider the following statistics:

• The result of zero tolerance policies has been an increase in both behavior problems and dropout rates (American Psychological Association Zero Tolerance Task Force, 2008).

• Public elementary and secondary schools in the United States assign 110,000 expulsions and 3 million suspensions each year, along with tens of millions of detentions (Children's Defense Fund, 2010; Dignity in Schools Campaign, n.d.).

• More than 2,467 U.S. students drop out of school each day (Children's Defense Fund, 2010).

The majority of teachers acknowledge that learning how to work with students, especially challenging ones, was not a main part of their education and that they thus feel overwhelmed by figuring out how to work with these students (Greene, 2008). Half of teachers leave the profession within the first four years, citing students with behavioral challenges and their parents as one of the main reasons (Public Agenda, 2004; Skiba, 2000). It's clear that we need to address this problem, but it's just as clear that a hard-line focus on discipline and control is not the right solution.

Why Do We Dismiss and Label Our Students?

The kids who enter our classrooms are *ours*—every single one of them. We must do whatever we can to keep them in our classrooms, in our schools, and in school—period. Leaving is not an option. How have we gotten to a place where we dismiss the students who challenge us—the ones who, very likely, need us most?

Many will cringe at the prospect of keeping all students in our classroom no matter what they throw at us, and I get it. Most educators want to find a way to help students succeed, but when students' destructive behaviors overwhelm us, our first instinct is to flee. Because we, as the adult teachers, cannot leave the situation, the logical solution seems to be to make the student leave so that we're able to return to our own level of regulation. Because we need to be in a regulated state to do our jobs, we do not take lightly those students who trigger us or threaten our sense of control over the classroom.

Many of us also feel the need to gain some understanding about the transgressing student before we believe we can effectively respond. When we feel overwhelmed by a student's behavior, we seek an explanation to help us comprehend why he or she is acting in such a manner. We reason that understanding will lead to a more effective response. And what's a more efficient, comprehensive way to understand something (or someone) than a name or a label? Of course, for students who have experienced trauma or have behavioral or other challenges, these labels are frequently deficit-based. Attention deficit hyperactivity disorder, oppositional defiant disorder, and others prime children's caregivers to define them by what they're missing. This deficit-focused orientation leads to unhealthy interactions and, often, students seeking inappropriate and disruptive ways to have their needs met.

Let me ask you a couple of questions that may evoke a strong reaction: who do you think has a greater need for a name or a label for a student—the student or the adult? Do we believe that a student needs a diagnosis to describe his or her behavior, or does the diagnosis fulfill our own need to attribute the behavior to a particular "cause"?

Our need for predictability is met when we have a means of understanding what is happening. When a student is acting in a perplexing way, having a label or a diagnosis assures us that the behavior is a result of something innate or developmental that we cannot control. So the behaviors, to this manner of thinking, aren't our fault.

Making students leave class and putting labels on them are both forms of dismissal that stem from our need for control. In both cases, we're allowing our own needs to trump our students' needs. We can do better.

Shifting Our Perspective

A frequent trigger for teachers is the perceived lack of control. Recently, I was reviewing the results of a survey initiated by a principal seeking staff feedback about school atmosphere, safety, and overall experience, and many of the "negative" comments stemmed from teachers' beliefs that they couldn't control student behavior or consistently enforce the school rules and that they were being overrun by disciplinary demands.

What would we discover if we dug deeper into the idea of control? What do we really control, anyway? Can we control whether the students in our classroom had a good night's sleep last night? Can we control whether they studied sufficiently for their exam? Can we control whether they fought with a parent or sibling, or whether they're worried about the well-being of a loved one? Can we control how students behave in school? When they're trying to stay regulated, often without helpful tools, their behavior is not under our control.

However, we can *influence* the situation dramatically. We can provide an environment that is safe and predictable. We can provide a caring, trusting relationship. We can help them remain focused on learning, despite the distractions. We cannot control everything, but we can influence quite a bit. And this is what trauma-affected students need from us.

Sit on Your Pockets!

About six years ago, I was working with an elementary school teacher named Ms. Jackson who was having a hard time accepting the fact that trauma can affect learning. Concerned about fairness, she was hesitant to adapt her environment for individual students. She believed strongly that all students should be treated equally and that they should follow her directions and make a choice to learn or not. She worried how her students and their parents might perceive her intentions if she altered her expectations. I actually agreed with much of what she said. My goal was simply to add this to her thinking: as educators, we have an obligation to truly understand how students learn and what may be affecting their capacity to learn.

One day, I was observing Ms. Jackson's class during circle time. She had set the expectation that all students must sit "on their pockets" before she would begin the read-aloud. On this particular day, a student named Amber preferred to sit on her knees. Although she was silent, Amber's alternative body positioning led to a disruption of the lesson. Several times, Ms. Jackson directed Amber to sit on her pockets; each time, the girl obliged, before eventually squirming back onto her knees. The teacher, assuming this was a deliberate act of defiance, refused to continue with the story, and a power struggle ensued. In the end, the school principal was called, and the "defiant" student was removed from class and taken to the office.

Later, when Ms. Jackson and I debriefed the situation, she was understandably upset that such a little thing had turned into a giant disruption. "Why couldn't she just sit on her pockets?" she lamented. "That sort of defiance is unacceptable in my classroom." Because I could see that Ms. Jackson was clinging to a label of "defiant," my first question was, "What would have happened if you had allowed her to sit on her knees?"

The longer we talked, the clearer it became that this wasn't about knees or pockets; it was about control. Neither party was willing to give up her sense of control: the well-intentioned teacher wanted to assert her authority and teach her students to adhere to the rules, and the student wanted to have some power and choice in her life. Both sets of needs are valid, although their responses were not conducive to a collaborative solution.

To help Ms. Jackson understand the complexity of the situation, I guided her through an investigation of Amber's reality, beginning with a discussion of what might be going on in her life: what if there were trauma or other not-OK factors in Amber's life? If Ms. Jackson were aware of this as a possibility, would her response to Amber change? Ms. Jackson began to recognize how Amber's possible experience of adversity may have led her to crave some control in the classroom situation. By viewing the disruption from Amber's point of view, Ms. Jackson was able to understand the behavior as need-based, not defiance-based.

We then looked at Ms. Jackson's response to the behavior. Why did she have such a strong reaction? As noted above, she held a strong belief that students should follow the teacher's directions. Amber's unwillingness to follow simple directions was a trigger that disrupted Ms. Jackson's ability to regulate. Armed with her new perspective, however, Ms. Jackson realized that she needed to leave some room for negotiation within the construct of classroom expectations and teacher authority. She and I worked out some strategies for ensuring that all students met the main expectations (in this case, respecting one another's right to listen and enjoy the story), while incorporating some "wiggle room" (being able to manage their own bodies in their own space). The strategies included offering students seating choices, coming up with the student job of page turner to support the learning environment, giving Amber a special chair to sit in, checking in with Amber before each transition, and offering Amber a stress ball to support her regulation and need for movement. Ms. Jackson owned her part in the classroom disruption and initiated a repair with Amber. Together, they revamped the circle-time expectations.

Shifting our thinking like this—looking at events through the student's eyes—takes courage and openness. Our need for control is a significant factor in how we define and interact with our students. I am grateful that I was able to witness the "pocket" confrontation with this educator and help her resolve the situation. No one was at fault here: student and teacher were doing the best they could with what they had in the moment. The good news is that we have the opportunity to learn from our experiences, whether positive or negative. The "bad" news is that we are always going to have new experiences to learn from!

PETE'S PRACTICE

I once worked with a veteran master teacher who frequently sent referrals to our behavior specialist and psychologist. When they asked Mr. Ramirez to sit down and strategize ways to help the students, he declined, saying, "I don't need strategies; I know how to manage my own classroom. I need you to test these kids to see what's going on with them. They're stealing the opportunity to learn from the other kids in the class."

When I sat down with Mr. Ramirez, I asked him Kristin's question: "Whose need would a label serve: the student's or yours?" One reality rang true: ultimately, regardless of the label or the diagnosis, the student would be back in class tomorrow, and it was the teacher's responsibility to ensure his or her healthy growth and learning. This, not surprisingly, uncovered the true issue at play for Mr. Ramirez: because he prided himself on a well-managed classroom, a disruptive student seemed to signal a weakness on his part. If he could chalk it up to a diagnosis, the kid's behavior would cease to be his fault. This was an issue of control and pride.

I followed up with some simple questions: "If a student struggles in reading, what do you do?" Mr. Ramirez responded with a list of interventions. "If a student struggles in math, what do you do?" He listed more strategies. "If a student struggles in behaving, what do you do?" After a moment, something sparkled in his eye. He realized that student conduct is something we must teach, meeting students where they are and moving them toward the identified standard. We don't need labels to understand students, just a willingness to see things from their point of view and a relentless drive to help them succeed.

I Can't... But I Can...

What if we started looking at the issue of control from a different angle? Rather than bemoaning the elements we cannot control, let's start focusing on the parts we can *influence*.

Here's an example of that thinking process in action: "I can't control that this student stole something out of my desk today, but I can control my emotional response to it... and I can learn to keep my door locked when I'm not in the classroom... and I can talk with the student to determine why he thought stealing from me was his best option... and I can influence him to take responsibility for his actions and repair with me."

Let's continue this train of thought: "I can't control that my administrator did not follow up with the student who stole from my desk, but I can control how I try to teach the student to see this from someone else's perspective… and I can talk with my administrator to find out why nothing was done to support me."

I have heard teachers respond to these suggestions by saying, "Oh, you don't know my administrator" or "That'd never work with this kid," but I believe that relationship, honesty, and a genuine interest in achieving success trump those excuses.

 Complete the following sentences (and any more you'd like to add) with your own truth, in your own words:

• I can't control whether _____ will come to my class today, but I can control . . .

• I can't control whether _____ passes this test, but I can control . . .

• I can't control whether _____ has experienced adversity and trauma at home, but I can control . . .

• I can't control whether we add _____ to our already-overloaded plates, but I can control . . .

Wrapping It Up

To some extent, names and labels are inevitable. After all, we all use adjectives to describe items, events, and people. Labels enable us to regulate ourselves: when we can predict and categorize what is in front of us, we feel more comfortable. Most of us don't teach with the intention of fixating on deficits, but we were trained to operate from that perspective.

An overreliance on labels does our students and ourselves a disservice. Instead of trying to pretend that need isn't there, let's refocus it by identifying which elements of a situation we can and can't control and then centering our energy on effecting positive change. This allows us to focus on the needs our students present, keeping us grounded in our cement shoes.

Reflective Questions

1.   Take a moment to think about a student you are currently struggling with, someone who really frustrates or irritates you. Picture this student in your mind and write down his or her name. What challenges does this student present? What choices does this student make that cause you distress? How do you typically respond to this student's behavior? What does a typical interaction between you two look like? How do you truly feel about this student? What sorts of emotions arise when you think about this student? Why do you think this is the case?

2.   Now look at the situation from the student's perspective. How do you think this student feels about you? How do you think this student feels about being in your classroom? If the student was asked how you feel about him or her, what do you think he or she would say? How would this student describe his or her interactions with you? What descriptors do you think this student would use to describe your relationship? Why do you think so?

3.   How do your responses to question 1 compare with those to question 2? Were you able to envision the student's perspective? How did it feel to look at your own behavior through someone else's eyes? Do you think you could hone this skill with more practice? How might shifting your perspective in this way change your relationships with the students (and even the adults) you work with?

10

Doors and Windows: Remembering to Explore All Options

When one door of happiness closes, another opens; but often we look so long at the closed door that we do not see the one which has been opened for us.

—Helen Keller

. . . .

How many times have you felt stuck with a student, trapped in a situation where you believed that the only option was to assert your authority, leverage your power, or otherwise act in a way that didn't align with your personal mission statement? Perhaps you've issued an ultimatum: *This is the last time I'm going to ask. If you don't do X right now, I'm going to do* Y. Maybe you are convinced that there is just one way to solve a certain problem, even when all evidence points to the contrary, so you keep trying the same thing to no avail. The problem with this approach is that you've effectively painted yourself into a corner.

I like to illustrate this phenomenon with a scenario. Let's say you've just entered a cabin in the woods, where you're supposed to meet your friends for a weekend getaway. As you escape the falling snow outside, the door closes behind you, and a mysterious lock latches into place. Try as you might, you cannot figure out the locking mechanism. You turn the doorknob and squeeze the lever, to no avail. So what do you do? You stop, sit and stare at the door for a moment, and then *do the very same thing*! Each time you try it, you think your perseverance will be rewarded and the door will magically open. As time goes on, you get increasingly frustrated with the door, pushing, pulling, kicking, and thumping on it until, lo and behold, a second mysterious lock latches into place. At this point, you are in your downstairs brain and have lost all power of reasoning. You are panicked, frustrated, and tired, and you just want the whole horrendous episode to be over. What you really needed to do in the first place was to step back, assess the situation, and analyze all the options available to you.

We need to do the same for the students and families we work with. Sometimes we get so bogged down by what is in front of us that we forget to look up and see alternative possibilities and solutions.

Finding a Window

When you were trapped in that cabin, you were fixated on the locked door as your sole means of escape. Had you stopped to assess all your options, you would have noticed a window. Remember: when you find yourself stuck and facing a locked door, there is always a window.

I think of the locked door as representing singular courses of action: kicking a student out of the classroom, issuing a failing grade, or shrugging our shoulders and giving up when our early efforts yield no perceivable benefit. At this point, we believe we've done everything we can, and evidently nothing will ever work to solve the problem.

When we arrive at that place where all we see is the door, this means we are exhausted, emotionally drained, and *done*. This response is our body's way of letting us know that we need to slow down, take a breath, and step away for a moment. This is when we need to take a break and seek some repair and rejuvenation so that we can summon the energy to find the windows.

Widen Your Peripheral Vision

When our vision becomes narrow, we go to our downstairs brain and leave our regulated state, which is where we need to be to logically explore our options. When you hit a wall (or a locked door), it's important to give yourself permission to step away and widen your peripheral vision so that you can see the windows. The following exercise, which I've used extensively in my practice and my trainings, is a powerful means of reconnecting to your upstairs brain.

Take a moment to get in a relaxed position, and fix your gaze on something that is directly in front of you. Now, as you concentrate on that object, simultaneously take into your vision an object that is on your left and an object that is on your right—for example, a door, a window, a picture, a plant, or a book. Maintaining your focus on the initial object, continue to widen the scope of your peripheral vision by scanning and acknowledging all those other objects to your left and right. Absorb the motions, the colors, and the items all around you. As you practice this exercise, you'll notice what's above and below the object of your focus, too.

As you widen your peripheral vision, your body will automatically give the signal to go back to your upstairs brain and give you permission to access the parts of your brain that are conducive to partnership and problem solving. Phew! The windows were there all along, and now you can access them.

Having the Patience Not to Eat the Chocolate

It can be hard to muster up the patience we need in this profession. We want instantaneous success. We want the intervention we choose to work the first time and to keep working throughout the course of the year. We don't want to spend endless hours trying to identify various ways to support a student's success. We often resort to a single set of interventions and accountability measures even when the students and staff they're meant to help don't improve.

Students, too, can be impatient. We watch them engaging in a cycle of self-destructive behavior while knowing that the outcome will not be positive, and we are baffled as to why they continue.

Even when we know that there are better ways of working or simply being, we all find ourselves reverting to old patterns. I like to think of this phenomenon in terms of chocolate: if we know that eating chocolate is bad for us, why do we continue to eat it?

In our society, we bombard people with interventions meant to deter them from eating the chocolate: jail, rehab centers, in-school suspension, detention, behavior plans, contracts, and so on. Many people succeed as long as they are surrounded by professionals who are invested in supporting that change. Yet eventually, those supports go away, and folks are left to their own devices. They must remember on their own how not to eat the chocolate. But what many of us fail to remember is that most of these people, including ourselves, have only ever known chocolate. Destructive or not, it has become comfortable and expected that we eat it.

For all of us, increasing our effectiveness or living healthier lives requires us to change, jettisoning our unproductive or even harmful practices for new, more potent ones. And truly changing a pattern of behavior or a way of being takes time, patience, and consistent support. We believe that a day, a few weeks, or even years of support in a structured setting will be enough to teach people to independently shun the chocolate, but I can assure you that *change is hard*! It doesn't happen overnight, and it rarely happens at the pace we want it to. We need to be committed in our efforts and trust the process. We also need to set realistic expectations for ourselves as well as for our students and families. We cannot ask for the moon when students have never even left the ground.

PETE'S PRACTICE

Early in my partnership with Kristin at the elementary school where I was principal, I conducted quite a bit of research about student behaviors, classroom management, and discipline. One resource I found particularly enlightening was Ross Greene's (2008) *Lost at School*. According to Greene, students who present behavior issues often actually have "lagging skills." He claimed that "kids will do well if they can"—that is, if students are struggling with something, it's likely because they simply lack the skills to address it appropriately.

In her work with us, Kristin took the stance that it was our collective responsibility to help students develop certain *competencies*, or skills that enable them to succeed across various contexts. Having this overarching mission helped us immensely. Our weekly Child Study Team meetings, which used to result in behavioral referrals or rigid discipline plans for students, became a time for us to examine the root causes of our students' struggles. What skills were they lacking? How could we help them develop those skills? How would we monitor their progress? With these questions guiding our work, the Child Study Team truly became an avenue for us to study our students, learn about them, and help them be successful.

As Pete's story illustrates, it is important to meet students where they are and to acknowledge their skills, habits, strengths, and needs. As we know, trauma exposure has detrimental effects on brain development, often delaying the acquisition of skills vital to survival. We have to believe that students are doing the best they can with what they have in the moment, and it is up to us to help them develop in areas where they have been deprived. This requires us to be flexible in our teaching methods, discipline approaches, and interactions with individual students. This is not an easy task, but it is essential if we want our students to grow and develop in healthy ways.

A Surprise Window in Math

I was working with a high school math teacher named Mr. Fitzgerald who happened to have one of my clients, Jamie, in his class. Neither teacher nor student was aware that I knew the other one, as confidentiality and HIPAA (the Health Insurance Portability and Accountability Act) discourage that kind of information exchange. For me, however, it was a gift to know both sides of the situation. The student had experienced some trauma and, as a result, had developed debilitating test anxiety. In addition, when he became overwhelmed, he tended to act out as a way of avoiding accountability and managing his stress. Mr. Fitzgerald took Jamie's actions personally, believing that Jamie's intention was to disrupt the class and prevent Mr. Fitzgerald from teaching. He described Jamie as "disrespectful." Jamie thought that Mr. Fitzgerald disliked him and went out of his way to make tests more stressful than necessary. He described his teacher as "mean."

Despite flunking every test, Jamie turned in flawless homework assignments. He explained that he understood the material but when it came time to take the tests, he would become overwhelmed and either walk out of the classroom (or get kicked out for his behaviors) or just sit and stare at the paper. He said, "I literally freeze and can't remember anything at all." Mr. Fitzgerald's take was that Jamie was probably copying another student's work for his homework assignments. During a staffing meeting with Mr. Fitzgerald, I asked whether it was possible that Jamie *did* know the math but was not a good test taker. I wondered if letting him take the test in a different way might prevent him from experiencing such high test anxiety.

Mr. Fitzgerald argued that this effort would create more work and be a waste of time. After acknowledging that that might be true, I said, "I know you have a strong desire to ensure that all your students are successful. What if a slight modification in the testing environment enabled this student to demonstrate his mastery of the learning standards? Would it be worth a shot?" After some further conversation and investigation into alternative assessment strategies, Mr. Fitzgerald agreed to let Jamie retake a math test during lunch, with some modifications. Together, they agreed that Mr. Fitzgerald would give the test orally and that Jamie could perform his computations and record his answers on a whiteboard. They also agreed that Jamie could explain his thinking as part of his responses.

Guess what happened? Jamie scored 100 percent. As they went through the test, Mr. Fitzgerald was so surprised by Jamie's knowledge that he wasn't quite sure how to proceed. Jamie, in turn, was so surprised by Mr. Fitzgerald's positive reaction that he, too, was in a state of shock. In the end, because the teacher was willing to seek out a window when all he'd ever known was the door, the student was able to demonstrate his knowledge.

Later, as Mr. Fitzgerald and I were discussing the results, he wondered how many students had been deprived of the opportunity to show their concept comprehension because they had trouble with the limited, traditional assessment methods he had used throughout his career. He wondered how many of his former students had histories of trauma, test anxiety, or some other hurdle that had prevented them from successfully meeting the requirements of the class. He vowed that he would begin teaching with a different mindset, to learn more about his students and their needs and be creative in how he assessed their mastery. His new insights and personal mission were a powerful commentary on his professional growth: once he looked away from the door, he noticed all the windows he had always ignored.

Here There Be Windows

The more we learn about our students, how the human brain learns, and the many ways we can teach (and reach) our kids, the better we can keep our students *engaged*—the third tenet of the whole child approach. Often, the strategies we prioritize work for the majority of our students—but as you know, the majority isn't "all." To reach some of our trauma-affected, struggling students, we have to think outside the box. We have to expand our professional repertoire to meet our students' individual needs. Sometimes we do this naturally, without even thinking about it. Other times, it takes quite a bit of contemplation and brainstorming to identify the approach that will reap the best benefit. Enlisting the support of a colleague or trusted partner to problem-solve can generate possibilities that we hadn't considered before.

Now take a moment and think about a time when you found a window for a student who was struggling. Maybe you allowed him to listen to music on his headphones while he took a test. Maybe you permitted her to complete an activity on the floor rather than at her desk. Maybe you agreed to meet a student's parent at a coffee shop for the parent-teacher conference because of the parent's aversion to the school environment (perhaps as a result of a past trauma)? Maybe you picked up a student in the morning and drove her to school, because without you she would have stayed home. Sometimes, it takes a departure from the norm to truly help a student learn.

Wrapping It Up

I know that you face many expectations and constraints and that you probably work tirelessly trying various ways to engage your students in learning. I also know that you may not get the validation and recognition you deserve for making these efforts. Such efforts are all examples of times when you found "windows" for your students. If it feels like an uphill battle at times, know this: countless people have told me that a past teacher's willingness to "find a window" for them changed their lives. Even if you don't believe your efforts are reaping much of a result, keep in mind that you're planting seeds. Although you may not get to see the flower bloom, your efforts may result in something extraordinary.

What are some of the ways you've gone above and beyond to help your students? Take a moment and acknowledge those experiences. Describe the one that sticks out for you the most.

Reflective Questions

1. Can you recall a time when you painted yourself into a corner and left yourself with only one door? What happened?

2. Consider the same scenario from the student's perspective. How did the situation play out for the student? How do you suppose the student felt during and after the interaction?

3. Are there some elements of your work that are "my way or the highway"? What are they? Why do you suppose you're committed to those approaches?

4. What do you notice when you engage in the "widen your peripheral vision" exercise on page 125? How might it help you in your professional responsibilities?

5. Have you ever thought of student misbehavior as symptomatic of "lagging skills"? If not, how might changing your mindset affect the way you interact with students who are misbehaving?

6.   Think of a trusted colleague or critical friend whom you can depend on to help you see the windows in your locked cabin. Does this person know how important he or she is to you?

7.   Think of a student who is struggling in your class right now. What approaches have you taken to encourage his or her success? Brainstorm with a trusted colleague some ways you might expand your options.

PART IV
Belief

Fear is not real. The only place that fear can exist is in our thoughts of the future. It is a product of our imagination, causing us to fear things that do not at present, and may not ever, exist. That is near insanity.... Do not misunderstand me. Danger is very real, but fear is a choice. We are all telling ourselves a story.

—Cypher Raige (played by Will Smith) in *After Earth*

. . . .

What story are you telling yourself? The way we interpret the events, people, and situations in our lives determines our reality. These interpretations are driven by our belief system. Our beliefs are the most powerful influence on the way we live, the choices we make, the relationships we have, the things we do, the places we go, and the dreams we keep.

As professionals in a caregiving field, we must be attuned to our belief systems. I've found, however, that people in general seldom look deeply into their own belief systems to understand the hidden motives behind how they think and what they do. Accordingly, Part IV of this book is an investigation into how our belief systems influence our thoughts and, by extension, our actions.

We start to peel the onion of our beliefs by considering what we truly believe about the young people we serve, particularly those affected by trauma. Although I advocate for a trauma-sensitive approach, I also insist that we hold all our students to a high standard of behavior, attitude, and achievement. The existence of trauma does not excuse our students from the rigors of *academic press*—that relentless push to excel in rigorous learning experiences. Rather, our knowledge of our students' trauma background offers us other avenues to connect with them so that they can continue to push and strive and excel.

I take a strength-focused approach, but even my Pollyannaish point of view has been challenged more times than I care to admit. There are days when I wonder if a student has been permanently scarred by his or her experiences and is truly lost, and I think that maybe there is nothing I can do to help this child. I'm guessing we have all found ourselves feeling that way about a particular student or person we know. It is scary but normal to feel hopeless and helpless at times and to worry that nothing we do can make a difference.

That said, I believe that a positive outlook on life and a belief in the inherent goodness of people are important and helpful to us in our work. My work with Pete and many other wonderful individuals aligns with that optimism. Seattle Seahawks quarterback Russell Wilson said it well: "I truly believe in positive synergy, that your positive mindset gives you a more hopeful outlook, and belief that you can do something great means you will do something great."

As you read the chapters in Part IV, believe in yourself and your students, and go do something great.

11

Forever Changed, Not Forever Damaged

You wanna fly, you got to give up the shit that weighs you down.

—Toni Morrison, *Song of Solomon*

. . . .

Trauma, whether complex or acute, affects us; this much we know. The intensity, duration, and impact of traumatic experiences, however, vary from situation to situation and from individual to individual. In any case, I believe that those of us who have experienced trauma are forever changed—not necessarily forever damaged. That part is up to us.

The phrase "forever changed, not forever damaged" is a powerful statement. I use it with my clients to help them validate the significance of their experiences and to empower them to determine the degree to which those experiences will affect their lives. I also use it in my consultation practices with schools, judges, medical professionals, probation officers, children's administrators—anyone who works with humans in a caregiving capacity—because we too often *do* view trauma-affected students and their families as "forever damaged."

Many victims of trauma do feel damaged by their experiences. They feel as if they will never be able to get over it and move on with their lives. It's not easy for them to give up the *stuff* that weighs them down. Accepting the realities of their experiences is a difficult challenge; some people allow the experiences to shape how they operate, with whom they interact—in fact, the very person they have come to be. Their histories of trauma become their script for current and future choices.

When you learn that someone you know has experienced trauma, do you look at him differently? Does his traumatic experience become the focus of your gaze, your perceptions, and your thoughts? Can you see him as separate from his trauma, or do you allow the trauma to define him? Do you view him as broken? Do you support his belief that he is broken?

If *you* have experienced some sort of traumatic event, how do you want others to see you? Would you like them to think immediately of your trauma experience, or would you prefer that they completely ignore it? Or do you fall somewhere in the middle? Do you want others to view you as forever damaged? As broken and incapable of healing?

How would this view empower anyone to do or be anything different?

Trauma as an Event, or Trauma as a Definition?

The degree to which trauma defines us varies for each individual. I have worked with people who never want to move past their trauma and feel a strong need to be validated for the hardships they have endured. I have worked with others who don't want their trauma to be acknowledged at all and who have worked their entire lives to ensure that it won't be. Regardless of how our trauma has affected us, we get to choose whether we will allow it to damage us forever.

I once worked with a young woman whose trauma history seemed inseparable from who she was and the choices she had made. She started counseling to see if there was "another way of being." As she processed her memories and grief, she got angry. She resented the fact that she had gone through so much hardship, and she was furious at the system for continually returning her to an abusive mother. She felt devastated that when she had finally been removed from her mother's care, she was placed with a woman who stripped away any opportunity for her to form an independent sense of self. The woman forced my client into a mold modeled on herself in a misguided effort to "save" the child from her years of abuse. As my client, then in her late 20s, started the process of independently defining herself, she had to examine those experiences and the influence they had on her development. She had heard me say, "Forever changed, not necessarily forever damaged; that part's up to you," and one day she just snapped and said, "You know, Kristin, you talk about forever changed and not forever damaged, but I *do* feel damaged. I feel like a piece of me was lost. Things were taken from me that I cannot get back, things I had no say in—my childhood."

As she worked through her anger and realization of her loss of innocence, she eventually had an epiphany: although her childhood differed from her vision of what a normal childhood was supposed to be, it had still been her childhood. It was her reality. And her adulthood sat before her, awaiting her choices and actions. Over time, she came to a place where she was able to say, "OK, maybe I'm not necessarily forever damaged." Getting to that place took a lot of hard work on her part, and I believe she still struggles with that acceptance. How could she not?

Pity and Low Expectations...

Can we look at our students without seeing them as "forever damaged"? It can be challenging when we are familiar with a student's trauma history; when we are intimately aware of the abuse, neglect, or traumatic events that our students have suffered, it all becomes more real to us. Empathy is a good thing, but all too often, I hear doubts about a student's learning capacity or ability to "overcome the odds" creep in, as though trauma equated directly with school failure, and I wonder who gave us permission to quit. Do we give up because we're afraid that this student's experience may be his or her truth? Are we afraid that we are not able to help, so quitting is our attempt to manage that overwhelming sense of hopelessness? How can we empower our students as well as ourselves to see their potential?

Can you identify your struggling students within the first month of school? If you work in an early learning environment, you are probably particularly attuned to which of your students will be the hardest to work with and who will struggle more in life. Can you look past these students' challenges, or at least leverage them as learning and growing experiences? Which do you see first, the deficit or the strength?

Many of us get hyper-focused on what happens during the 14 to 18 hours our students aren't with us. We feel frustrated by the choices that students' caregivers make and by what can feel like blatant sabotage of all the hard work we are doing in school. Sometimes we experience a sense of utter helplessness that threatens to destroy our motivation to keep going. So I want you to stop and think about the 6 to 10 hours you *do* have with those students. I want you to focus on the amazing things you can accomplish in those hours, because that is what you can control. We have an incredible opportunity in this period to show students what they are capable of, to expose them to different ways of being, to teach them healthy ways of managing, to empower them to learn and grow in productive ways, and to love them both for who they are and for who they may become.

... Or a Focus on Strengths and Potential?

Once we identify our students who struggle, how can we help them heal and develop in ways that will set them up for success? Can we focus on our students' strengths rather than their deficits? Can we view our students as overflowing with potential rather than doomed to failure? It's up to us.

What would it look like if we shifted our efforts from focusing on students' struggles to developing their strengths? At the end of each day, do you fixate on the mistakes you made, the work you didn't accomplish, and the unpleasant interaction you had with a colleague or student? Or do you end the day with gratitude, affirmation, and a little toast to your accomplishments? Which is more helpful? According to research, a positive mindset would help you feel happier, more satisfied with work, and more patient as well as lead to an increased willingness to help others and try new things. Sounds like something worth pursuing.

One of my favorite movie scenes comes from *Moneyball* (you can view it at https://www.youtube.com/watch?v=xn7C6jgl0RI) and features Oakland A's catcher Jeremy Brown's famous home run. Brown has convinced himself that he could never run all the way to second base on a well-batted ball. His negative self-image, an incarnation of the idea of being "forever damaged," seems to consume him. When he hits a long drive, he knows he should go for the double, but he slips rounding first base. Was his fall subconscious self-sabotage? Was it a result of his self-imposed limits? He scrambles back to first base in the hope that he hasn't caused an out for his team. He seems surprised when the first base coach and even players from the other team encourage him to get up and continue running. It takes seconds before he even realizes that he had hit a home run over the fence.

Many of us, along with our students, develop a notion that "I can't," "I'm too stupid," or "I will never be good enough." Trauma-affected individuals sometimes use their trauma as a rationale for imposing low expectations on themselves or dismissing the idea of achieving success. That negative self-talk sometimes overrides our capacity to recognize the times when we *do* succeed. It can make us blind to the home runs that our students and we ourselves are hitting. It gets in the way of our ability to see the good in ourselves and in others.

Take a moment and think about some "home runs" that you and your colleagues have hit this year. What unexpected strides did you make? Did you exceed your own expectations at all? Write down some of these key professional accomplishments.

Now it's time to help some of the students you work with to begin identifying their own "home runs." Acknowledging successes increases the likelihood that they will recur, and by highlighting students' strengths and potential, we may be able to help them see themselves in the same light. Together, we can shift students' self-perception of brokenness and inadequacy to high expectations and an awareness of their strengths.

The better we know our students, the more effective this approach will be. For now, think about a student who has a significant trauma history; has low self-esteem; struggles with attendance, behavior, or coursework; and seems to believe that he or she is "forever damaged." Think about his or her story. Does he or she have a high ACE score?

Think about a student who is troubled or is struggling in school in some way. Reflect on the work you have done with this student thus far, and answer the following questions:

1. What are the strengths of this student? What is he or she good at?

2. What are the interests of this student? What does he or she enjoy doing?

3. What is meaningful to this student?

4. What motivates this student?

5. How do you typically feel about this student? (Be honest!)

6. Who is the student most connected with at school?

7. When does this student tend to be most successful at school?

8. When this student struggles, what do you think he or she needs? What might he or she be asking from you?

9. What forms of praise does this student respond best to?

Now start to think of a way to engage this student with you and others in the building, including other students and adults. How can you help this student see him- or herself as lovable and worthwhile, recognize his or her own potential, create opportunities to be success-ful, and make academic gains?

The following questions will support you in developing a plan to help this student:

1.   What strategies have you used that worked with this student?

2.   What strategies have you used that did not work?

3.   Have you shared the effective strategies with others in the building who are also struggling to connect with this student?

4.   Can this student recognize when he or she made a healthy choice? Do you praise this student when he or she is on task and working to his or her potential?

5.   Give some examples of strategies you can use that will engage the student with you in a positive way.

6.   What supports do you need to feel successful with this student? Whom can you rely on to provide that support?

7.   Name three ways you plan to connect with this student in a different way this coming week.

8.   What are some ways you plan to try connecting with the student's family?

9.   What are some positive ways to engage this student with his or her peers?

The students who give us the greatest challenges are often those who provide us with the greatest rewards. If we are willing to view our students through a wider whole child lens rather than a narrow deficit-focused mindset, we can see many options for supporting our students. The fourth tenet of the whole child approach is to ensure that each student has access to personalized learning and is *supported* by qualified, caring adults. Differentiating instruction to meet each student's readiness, interests, and learning preferences (Tomlinson, 2014) is a terrific start. Clarifying learning goals, providing consistent encouragement, and providing every student with a mentor add significant value (Brown, 2008). Taking the time to build a strong relationship, demonstrating empathy, and engaging with each student as an individual human being will further propel us along this path.

PETE'S PRACTICE

As a school principal, I often had parents drop in to talk with me about their children. One such parent, Tina, stopped by to let me know that her impending divorce was especially difficult emotionally for her youngest daughter, Alicia, an incoming 7th grader at my school. Tina wanted her daughter's teachers to be aware of the situation so that they could alert the school counselor when she was having a particularly rough day.

The teachers absorbed and applied this information in different ways. One, with the best of intentions, felt sorry for Alicia and saw her as a victim. When Alicia didn't participate in class or complete all her homework, the teacher chalked it up to Alicia's tumultuous home life and let the "sweet little thing" off the hook. Another teacher offered Alicia additional leadership responsibilities within the classroom: collecting assignments, helping to prepare lesson materials, tutoring classmates who were struggling, and offering advice on choices for text selections. Guess where she flourished? Was she the poor kid whose dad beat her mom and abandoned them? Or was she the resilient, kindhearted young lady who ended up volunteering to lead the school's antibullying efforts?

As adults and professionals, our expectations for our kids are incredibly powerful. The way we see our students—through a strength-focused lens or in a deficit-based model—shapes our beliefs, and our expectations follow suit. Alicia taught me and the teachers with whom she worked a valuable lesson that forever changed doesn't necessarily mean forever damaged.

Wrapping It Up

Originally, as I was writing this section, I had intended it to frame the way we, as adults and professionals, view our students—particularly those with a known trauma history. Interestingly, the approaches I describe are equally effective for adults to clarify their own identities. Once we are open, honest, and generous with ourselves, we are more available to our students. This is a common theme in this chapter, in this book, and in our work with youth. Although it's not all about us, creating a trauma-sensitive learning environment begins with us.

Reflective Questions

1. What is the first thought that comes to your mind when you are told, "This young person has experienced a significant amount of trauma"?

2. Are you conscious of other people's trauma histories once you're made aware of them? How does that knowledge affect your thinking?

3. How would you explain the phrase "Forever changed, not forever damaged" to a friend or colleague?

4. What attributes do you think a person must have to "soldier on" and overcome the negative effects of trauma?

5. Have you ever heard a colleague diminish a student's potential because of the hardships in the student's life? How did you respond? Did you say anything? How did you advocate for the student?

6. What is the difference between being strength-based and deficit-based? Which approach do you identify with when you see yourself and others? How do you know? How does this affect your relationships with and perceptions of others?

7. What step can you take today to encourage and motivate a student who is downtrodden and feeling the weight of the world?

12

It's OK to
Be Not-OK

My thoughts are all I got, so I try to make 'em brave.

—Jason Mraz, "Hello, You Beautiful Thing"

. . . .

In Chapter 11, we discussed the fact that although trauma may leave a lasting imprint on our spirit, it doesn't need to render us incapable of moving forward. We must validate and reconcile ourselves to our trauma history, yet we needn't be governed by it. We have power in determining the degree to which trauma will define our lives and ourselves. That said, no one should feel pressured to "just get over it." It takes time to work through grief, hurt, and traumatic experiences—longer for some than for others. And that's OK. There is no "one size fits all" when it comes to healing.

I recently worked with a 16-year-old girl who had been sexually abused for many years by a family member, and she was frustrated with herself for not being able to move on. I can't help wondering when it became so important to be "fine." **It's OK to be not-OK.** The healing process begins with our willingness to give ourselves permission to grieve our traumatic experiences. Once we truly connect with what happened to us, we can reach a level of acceptance that enables us to move forward in a healthy way.

Making Meaning

We humans have a need to make meaning from our experiences. We crave a way to make sense of our world and put our life events into context. This process prepares us to make decisions in the future. Viktor Frankl's (1946) *Man's Search for Meaning*, a book chronicling his experiences in Nazi death camps during World War II and describing the psychotherapeutic method he subsequently developed to help himself and others find a positive purpose in life, provides an incredible example of this process.

Having a secure attachment to a trusted "safe person" can help us and our students process our emotions and experiences. Yet many of us, along with the majority of our trauma-affected students, do not have such an attachment. We're left to our own devices to explore the not-OK events of our lives and understand how they shape the way we make decisions. All of us, students and adults alike, are doing our best with what we have, which doesn't necessarily lead to the healthiest or safest choices. Finding someone in our lives whom we can connect to and feel safe with makes all the difference in honing our ability to learn from our experiences and move forward in healthy and meaningful ways.

I was working with a teacher in my clinical practice who had a significant trauma history. She truly was a gifted "kid whisperer," masterfully attuned to the needs of her students. However, she was not nearly so well attuned to her own needs. She worked diligently to identify the templates she had developed because of her trauma history and realized that her self-concept included beliefs like "I am not lovable" and "People will eventually want to leave me." Unconsciously, she had developed a pattern of sabotaging relationships.

Through our sessions and her own hard work, she finally began to see herself as lovable. She began to trust herself and her husband more deeply and to take risks, emotionally, in her relationship. Exploring the not-OK events of her life allowed her to understand her decision-making templates—after all, disagreeing over what color to paint the walls wasn't a cause for divorce!—and create new ones that better aligned with who she really was. This process took time, concerted effort, and more than a few tears, but it led her to some life-changing breakthroughs.

PETE'S PRACTICE

Some years back, I worked with a remarkable 2nd grade teacher who exerted himself tirelessly to educate every student who crossed his path. Mr. Pargaduiza was teaching in the lunch line, in the hallways, on the playground, and in the neighborhood grocery store. Students didn't need to be in his class to benefit from his tutelage.

More impressive, however, was his ability to connect with others— to empathize with them and to encourage them to work harder, keep trying, believe in themselves, and conquer all obstacles. He insisted that every individual was capable of greatness.

Only after working with him for two years did I hear his story: a product of a broken home, Mr. Pargaduiza had battled not one but two types of cancer and endured a horrific car crash. He didn't talk openly about these experiences, although they were clearly a big part of his life and a contributing factor to whom he had become. He had every reason to feel beaten down, but instead, he was one of the most optimistic, energetic human beings I've ever encountered. Like many who knew him, I was inspired by him and have emulated the way he interacted with his fellow travelers. In his own way, he had discovered a way to be OK with his not-OK.

Acknowledge the Not-OK

We can better help our students if we work through our own not-OK. The first step is the most difficult: acknowledging our reality. Let's start with work, which is often a cause of stress and anxiety. Give yourself permission to acknowledge what is not-OK about your job. What are you unhappy about? What is causing you worry or frustration? What is challenging your confidence? Are there things that make you not want to go to work some mornings?

Write down three things that make success and happiness at work more difficult. What makes you want to hit the "snooze" button and crawl back under the covers for the day?

1.

2.

3.

How did this exercise feel? Is your anxiety level rising or diminishing? Now try this follow-up exercise: imagine writing those three stressors on a notecard that you wear around your neck at work. How would that feel? How might your feelings change if all your colleagues were doing the same thing, so everyone's stressors were visible at all times? Would it be embarrassing? Validating? Would you expect to see some of your stressors also written on your colleagues' cards? Do you think your colleagues' cards would include stressors that you had not considered but could relate to?

Becoming Vulnerable

In my group trainings, I lead participants in a variation on the activity just described. There are two reasons for this exercise: first, it requires folks to become vulnerable. (I'll get to the second reason in the next section.) This can be very difficult because it puts us at risk. It forces us to acknowledge what's not-OK about our jobs, which are often an integral part of our lives. But by doing so, we are granting ourselves permission to move to a place that supports healing and growth. Our society overwhelms us with messages to bury our hurt, to pretend that it doesn't exist, to be devoid of emotion, or to take a pill to "fix" it. (Don't get me wrong; I am a supporter of healthy and ethical use of medication, but it's not a panacea for everything not-OK in our lives.) Ultimately, we need to allow ourselves to have *normal reactions to not-OK things*. For some, this takes healing, support, understanding, and time.

Over the years, I have worked with a special family whom I feel blessed to know. The parents lost their son unexpectedly a few years ago and have had a hard time dealing with their loss, as you might imagine. One day, I was talking with the dad. He reflected on his continued struggle to accept that his son was no longer on this earth. He said, "You know, I still find myself buying Doritos at the store. It has been three years since he died, and I'm still buying Doritos. And the bitch of it is, no one else in the family even likes Doritos." He is going to laugh that I put this in the book, but his comment has stayed with me in a way that others have not. It gave me a powerful insight into the reality of this man's life. He has endured excruciating pain, and as he continues to process those events, he's struggling to "move forward" in the way that society expects him to. In that moment, I thought to myself, *Yeah, it's OK to be not-OK.*

Our Students Are Vulnerable, Too

The second reason for the "stressor cards" exercise is to help us understand what it might feel like for our students to be vulnerable with us. We expect them to come to school every day and immediately do two things: (1) trust us and (2) enter the learning mode. We ask them to leave their baggage at the door and enter our domain, setting aside whatever stressors they have in *their* lives so that they can be successful at what *we* need them to do. Further, we expect them to provide us with their personal information and to share with us their deepest secrets—not so that we can help them manage the lasting effects of those events, but so that we can understand how to help them "put it aside" for learning's sake. We expect them to open up to us and to explain, when applicable, why they cannot perform the way we want them to. We assume that they will see us as safe and trustworthy despite our own ignorance of their truth. Sometimes, what they really need is to have permission to be not-OK. The question for us is, *How can we grant them that permission and provide a safe place where they can just be not-OK?*

Educators and caregiving professionals across the country tend to meet that question with predictable skepticism. The education train doesn't slow down just because a student has experienced trauma; the expectations for learning, behavior, and overall growth remain constant. By no means do I advocate halting the education process to allow a student to become stagnant with grief. Rather, we must find ways to support one another—students and teachers alike—through such experiences. We must strive for a balance between taking the time to mourn the losses associated with traumatic experiences and finding ways to manage life's everyday expectations. For example, you could tell a struggling student, "I will hold your worry for you for now, because it will still be there at the end of the day. I think you could use a break from that worry, and I would love to see how you can challenge your upstairs brain today." Or you could recruit a colleague who shares an interest with your struggling student to offer "visit moments." A 3rd grade teacher I know who was also an artist agreed to be the safe person for a student who loved to draw. When the student struggled in his own class, he came to this teacher's classroom—without interrupting the lesson—and, in between directives, the teacher engaged the student in drawing. Within 10 minutes, this student would be ready to return to his own classroom and reengage in the learning—all because this school's staff agreed to work as a team.

Our capacity to acknowledge and attend to personal difficulties while still working toward expectations is often defined as *resilience*. Resilience can be learned and practiced; it is not a genetic trait that we inherit. The Mayo Clinic Staff (n.d.) writes this about resilience:

> When you have resilience, you harness inner strength that helps you rebound from a setback or challenge, such as a job loss, an illness, a disaster or the death of a loved one. If you lack resilience, you might dwell on problems, feel victimized, become overwhelmed or turn to unhealthy coping mechanisms, such as substance abuse.
>
> Resilience won't make your problems go away—but resilience can give you the ability to see past them, find enjoyment in life and better handle stress. If you aren't as resilient as you'd like to be, you can develop skills to become more resilient.

We all demonstrate our resilience in different ways. Access to healthy support systems and safe environments augment the development of resilience. Relationships matter. Professional educators—teachers, counselors, administrators, and others—can provide the environment, the relationship, and the support systems for our trauma-affected students and families.

Managing the Not-OK

We've all had those days: our alarm didn't go off, a crisis occurs, the coffee stand was closed, those pants just didn't fit right, the meeting started seven minutes ago, a loved one argued with us... the list could go on and on. When the stress piles up, you're experiencing a traumatic event, or life is otherwise beating on you, what do you do?

 Think about how you manage your own not-OK. Whom do you seek out? Where do you go? Do you have a ritual or routine that you rely on to get you through the mess?

Now think about the students you work with. What do you provide for them when they are not-OK? Do you have a safe place in your classroom setting? Have you established a ritual or routine that they can look forward to? How do you communicate "You are safe with me" to your students?

Safe People

It is crucial for us all to have "safe people" in our lives. These are the folks we trust with our very lives. We count on them, we seek them out, and we lean on them. Having a safe person is an essential component for fostering resilience. One person often isn't enough. In fact, it helps to build an "inner circle," with one safe person for each major sphere of our life: professional, personal, and spiritual. These people truly *know* us, *understand* us, and still want to be there *for* us unconditionally. They love us despite—and sometimes because of—our flaws.

I can attest to the value of having a "safe person" in my professional and personal sphere, someone who empathizes with the stresses of my work, who can be present with me when I need to celebrate a small victory or mourn a regretful moment. My safe person is my best friend, Laurie. She gets me like no other, and, as a bonus, she is also a counselor, which helps tremendously.

Here's an example of how much Laurie helps me. Several years ago, I was providing a series of trauma-informed care trainings to a number of schools in my hometown. I was working long hours and was stretched pretty thin. In the midst of this, my daughter's 5th grade teacher passed away unexpectedly. Although my daughter was in 8th grade at the time, she was still at the same school and was fond of this teacher. She was devastated, along with the rest of the community. The teacher's funeral was to take place on the same day that I was scheduled to present at a school where I hadn't worked before with teachers I hadn't met. The funeral was at 1:00, and the training was scheduled to begin at 3:00. Because of my schedule and contract obligations, I could not reschedule the training. We somehow managed to find a way for me to fulfill my commitment for the training while being able to attend the funeral with my daughter to honor this incredible woman's life.

Laurie, who was aware of this situation, knew that I would probably be emotional and frazzled heading into the training, so she took it upon herself to call the school counselor at that school and ask her to help me out. When I raced through the doors of the school, a woman I had never met stood before me. She said, "Pretend I am Laurie." She gave me a gigantic hug, handed me a water bottle, and said a few words on behalf of Laurie that would help me. It was exactly what I needed at the time. Having someone I trusted know my current state and find a way to access support for me enabled me to refocus and provide a solid training for the attendees.

I cannot overstate the importance of having a safe person, or a robust inner circle of safe people, in developing a healthy approach to life and providing some security and comfort for when things go awry.

Wrapping It Up

Educators often end up filling many roles beyond their job descriptions. When students call with broken hearts, dampened spirits, and a trauma-affected reality, educators heed that call. We have to. Often, school is the safest place for students to grieve, to heal, to be not-OK, and to learn how to be OK with their not-OK. Forging strong relationships with caring, committed adults is a powerful step in the healing process. It's up to us to provide the safe environment and healthy atmosphere in which that relationship can take hold.

Reflective Questions

1. Who is in your inner circle? Do you have a trusted go-to person (or go-to people) in your professional, personal, and spiritual spheres?

2. Why have you gravitated toward (or chosen) these individuals? What makes them "safe" to you?

3. Have you communicated your appreciation to these people? How might you tell them how much they mean to you?

4. Consider the students in your class or school. How can you begin the conversation to help them identify their inner circle of safe people?

5. Does every single student have a safe person in the school? How might you find out?

6. How could you ensure that the adults in your school are "safe people" for every student, thereby allowing students to select those who they believe best understand them and can help them process their emotions?

7. How can we teach resilience to our students to help them manage their not-OK?

13

Don't Let Fear Drive the Bus

Children have not changed. Childhood has. The children around us are merely reflecting the challenging, sometimes scary changes in their environment and world.

—Barbara Oehlberg, *Making It Better*

. . . .

Every generation tends to lament the incorrigible nature of the next generation's youth. The words "Kids today" are rarely followed by a series of gushing compliments. The assumption is that with each passing generation, the makeup and behaviors of our children are not just different, but also worse. I like to challenge this assumption, so I frequently ask the folks I'm working with to examine the rationale for their thinking. Have children *really* changed? Are our kids actually less respectful or more troublesome than we were? How can we even know? What metrics are we using to measure those characteristics?

Invariably, upon reflection, people revise their viewpoints at least slightly. The most common revelation is that kids will be kids, but the world they live in has changed. When pressed to describe *how* the world is different, the most common response is that "we know more." Because of the Internet, the 24-hour news cycle, social media, and a gazillion lines of communication, information from every conceivable source or point of view is shared instantaneously. Everything is accessible, everyone is connected, and, because we know what *does* happen almost immediately—and because the media portray these events dramatically—we gravitate toward thinking about the dangerous and scary things that *could* happen. The not-OK begins to seem omnipresent.

The Good Old Days

Do you ever reminisce about your own childhood? For many, childhood was a time to be outside for hours at a time, playing and riding bikes and chasing butterflies and partaking in all kinds of adventures. I often laugh about how my friends and I went home only to "pee, poop, or eat." Otherwise, we were often gone for most of the day, without parental supervision. We used to spend hours playing in a ravine or on a tree swing in the middle of the woods, or biking several miles to the store to buy candy.

Throughout all of those experiences, I never felt scared or worried that something "bad" would happen to my friends or me. My childhood was consumed by a sense of innocence. From a child's perspective, life is a grand adventure. A crack in the sidewalk is something to step over so you don't "break your mother's back," not something you could trip on that might result in a broken wrist and six weeks in a cast. Yet when I work with parents today, fear is often the driving factor of their decisions. They admit that their fear of something dangerous happening influences their decisions to allow or forbid their children to do certain things. Many say, "I hate feeling this way, but I am not willing to take the risk."

Is Fear Driving Our Bus?

J. Eric Gentry, an internationally recognized leader in the study and treatment of traumatic stress and compassion fatigue, shared this comment at a workshop I attended some years back: "We are the safest generation to ever live on this planet, yet we are the most afraid."

Why is this the case? Is it because of social media and instant access to information? Is it because our perspective has changed? Is there another reason? Was I safer growing up in the 1970s, or was I just blissfully unaware of the danger that lurked behind every corner? Did I just not know about all the not-OK things that *could* happen to me? Now, as a parent myself, am I letting my awareness of the horrible events of the world influence how I limit my kids' freedoms?

In other words, am I letting fear drive my bus? In my clinical practice, I often ask my clients this question to determine what is motivating their decision-making processes. I do know this: when fear drives, we go nowhere good. In fact, many in our field believe that not exposing children to some level of risk does them a disservice. Without risk exposure, children are deprived of the opportunity to learn how to manage the intensity associated with risk and, as a result, may be set up for the possibility of even greater harm.

Sheltering children from risk and steering them away from possible stressors won't protect them in the end; at worst, our well-intentioned fear of the not-OK may ruin their childhood and sabotage their future. If we limit children's ability to experiment and explore, how will they develop their self-concept and self-confidence? How will they gain the skills associated with independence, creative play, problem solving, and critical thinking? Developmentally, children's feelings of competence—including the ability to tolerate stress, identify strengths, accomplish tasks, and develop self-worth—stem from learning, growing, experimenting, stumbling, and getting up again. If our goal as parents is to raise and nurture independent, competent future citizens, how will our fear affect our long-term ambitions?

It is important that we *all* learn how to deal with stress and develop a tool set to help us manage the mess that comes with life. Instead of bubble-wrapping our children, we need to teach them the skills to manage crises in a way that empowers them.

Fear in the Classroom

This same priority applies to educators, since we have the charge of raising and nurturing other people's children for six or more hours each day. How much does fear influence our decisions, responses, beliefs, and interactions in the classroom? Considering all the pressure piled on teachers, the stress associated with such a massive responsibility, and the challenges that students present, it's no wonder we sometimes hand the keys to our bus over to fear.

Consider Zach, a 9-year-old with a history of acting out at school. He was well known for hitting, kicking, throwing tantrums, and, eventually, ending up in the principal's office or being sent home. Everyone on the teaching staff had heard the tales of his outbursts, and many worried that they would escalate as he got older. His teacher, Ms. Rinzler, shared her fear that his acting out might hurt someone and completely disrupt her classroom. In consultation with me, she admitted to capitulating to Zach and compromising her own values in an effort to prevent his outbursts. She was tired and overwhelmed, and her own sense of competency had taken a hit. She found herself hoping that Zach would have a sick day or get suspended or that his family would move to another school district "so I can have peace again in my classroom."

Ms. Rinzler and I discussed how her fear of Zach acting out influenced her responses, behaviors, and overall competency as an educator. She admitted to "waiting for him to misbehave." In essence, by trying to create a sense of predictability, she set a subconscious expectation of his misbehavior. We examined the way her fear had resulted in a self-fulfilling prophecy and discussed what might happen if she stopped worrying about the possibility of Zach acting out. What would happen if he didn't act out? What would the classroom look and feel like? What happened when he *did* comply with classroom standards? Could she remember a time when he had?

PETE'S PRACTICE

At the middle school where I was principal, we spent a great deal of time discussing best instructional practices. We did our best to ensure that every classroom offered every student an optimal learning environment, and teachers structured their lessons to increase student engagement.

Yet in one math classroom, I always seemed to encounter the teacher lecturing in the "drill-and-kill" format. In our discussions, the teacher, Mrs. Rice, professed to believe in the various student engagement strategies but claimed they wouldn't work in her classroom. "I have too many students struggling with the material, which causes them to misbehave," she told me. "If I hand the reins over to the students, the class will be chaos. This structure works for them because they stay under control."

As we talked further, it became evident to her that the structure indeed worked for her, because it was predictable. We discussed the possibility that controlling a classroom is an illusion and dug into the deeper motivation behind her decisions. Ultimately, she realized that fear was driving her bus: she was afraid of losing control of the class and worried that "left to their own devices," students wouldn't learn. I paired her with one of our instructional coaches, who helped her implement some simple strategies that provided structure in a more engaging manner. Soon, with some trial and error, lots of feedback, and a partner to help her work through her own "messiness," Mrs. Rice was able to confidently apply several engagement strategies. When reviewing her end-of-year data, she was surprised by how much her students had grown academically. "I had no idea we could make this much progress," she confided. "Maybe students exceeding my expectations was what I was really afraid of."

How Do We Handle Fear?

Let's examine how we handle fear. Take a moment and reflect on your current role as a professional. Think of your expectations, professional relationships, goals, and overall sense of safety. When you are faced with a disruptive student, do your thoughts run along the same lines as the following?

> *Go ahead, young man; eat the crayon. If that will keep you quiet and nondisruptive for a little while, I don't mind one bit.*

If you do tend toward this attitude, you might find yourself rationalizing it:

> *Crayons are nontoxic these days. What harm can it really do if I let him eat it? I mean, it's just a crayon, and maybe now we can proceed with our writing lesson without a major disruption.*

As simple and silly as this scenario appears, you may relate to it. Our fatigue from dealing with repeated disruptions and our fear that they will recur influence the choices we make with regard to this student and his well-being. Clearly, eating the crayon is not in the student's best interest. How do we intervene? What strategy might redirect the student toward the writing lesson? How might we avoid a blowup and simultaneously address the crayon issue? How might we be more proactive in preventing such scenarios from arising? These are the questions we should be asking ourselves, no matter how much they exhaust us. The following exercise will walk you through a series of questions that will prompt you to explore your professional fears.

Let's examine the degree to which fear affects your overall sense of self and feelings of competency. Rate the statements presented below on a scale of 1 to 5.

No Effect	Small Effect	Moderate Effect	Significant Effect	High Effect
1	2	3	4	5

1. I worry that my students' scores on the current standardized tests will influence my overall job performance rating. _____

2. I worry that as I begin to teach more, my sense of organization and competency seems to be deteriorating. I believe that I am less effective than I used to be. _____

3. There is at least one student in my classroom who can be disruptive and affects my ability to teach effectively. _____

4. I worry that the current evaluation standards will affect my ability to keep teaching. _____

5. There is a student who I am or have been afraid of. He or she affects (or affected) my feelings of competency as a professional. _____

6. There is a parent who I am or have been afraid of. He or she affects (or affected) my feelings of competency as a professional. _____

7. I worry that a student or professional I know is so upset that he or she is contemplating and may attempt suicide. _____

8. I worry or think about being sued as a professional. _____

9. I shy away from confrontation with colleagues and peers. _____

10. I do not like to be challenged by others. _____

11. I avoid speaking up at meetings because of how I might be interpreted by others. _____

12. I worry if a student or colleague doesn't like me. My desire to be liked influences the way I interact with others. _____

13. I worry that I will not meet standards. _____

14. I worry that I will not provide the students I am responsible for with what they need. _____

15. I worry when people judge my work and ability as a professional. _____

16. With all of the changes in education and expectations of staff, I worry that I will not be successful in my job. _____

17. I find paperwork and menial tasks getting in the way of my ability to do good work. _____

18. When a student appears sad or withdrawn, I avoid approaching him or her because I am afraid of what he or she might say. _____

19. I avoid calling a parent because I worry that he or she may become angry with me for what I have to say. I put off making those calls because I'm afraid of how parents may react to the information.

_____

Fact Versus Fear

Identifying the role of fear in our lives and acknowledging its influence on our decision-making process is an important first step. The next step is to reduce fear's influence by altering the way we view each situation, which means separating fact from fear. Distinguishing between the two is a challenging but crucial step. Then we need to figure out how much we base our decisions on fear versus fact.

Let's return to the crayon-eating scenario. These are the facts of the matter:

- The student is eating a crayon. This is not healthy.
- He is usually disruptive, and his crayon consumption is not disrupting the class.
- The teacher has not addressed the crayon issue.

The larger context is likely to be more complicated than that, but let's leave it there for now. The teacher has opted to ignore the crayon eating out of fear that a confrontation may escalate the student's behavior. The teacher is therefore viewing this scenario based on what *might* happen instead of what *is* happening. With a little investigation, the teacher might learn what is motivating the student's behaviors, and knowing the motivation will enable the teacher to take the appropriate step:

- Is the student nervous about the lesson? *Invite the student to join the group when he is ready.*
- Is the student feeling ignored and in need of attention? *Recruit the student into an active role, such as delivering handouts, checking the pencils, or calling on volunteers to share.*
- Is the student challenged by writing? *Assure the student that he will get some one-on-one assistance after the whole-class introduction.*
- Is the student expecting the teacher to reprimand him? *Instead, compliment (in advance) his decision to join the class.*

Not surprisingly, many of our trauma-affected students have the same bus driver: fear. The more we know about their situations and trauma history, the more fear we may feel for them, too. In fact, our concern for their safety can disrupt our own functioning and coping strategies. We may even begin to feel a certain hopelessness, which may result in diminished expectations and a reluctance to interact with students in the way we were professionally trained to. In these cases, it's important for us to clarify the facts of the matter and to allow the facts—not the fear—to determine our course of action.

Wrapping It Up

In my experience, it's been confirmed time and time again that education professionals care about students and want to help them succeed by keeping them *challenged*—the fifth tenet of the whole child approach. It's also been confirmed that educators can get caught up in the issues we wish did not exist: disruptive or uninterested students, disengaged families, and disrespectful behaviors. When we focus on these negative elements, the *fear* of their presence influences our decision making. When we see a student as a tornado waiting to happen rather than a child who needs guidance and instruction, we're letting fear drive our bus. The challenge is to shift our focus and set the table with positive expectations for every child in every situation. In other words, give the bus keys to the facts.

Reflective Questions

I encourage you to pair up with a trusted colleague or friend and share and compare your answers to the following questions. You may be surprised by how validating the process is.

1. What's driving your bus? How do you know?

2. What was your childhood like? If you are a parent, how does your childhood compare with your children's childhood? If you are a teacher, how does it compare with your students' childhood?

3. What risks do you expose your children or students to? How do you help them navigate those experiences?

4. Do you have students who you continually expect will misbehave? Do you find yourself just waiting for them to misbehave? Do you sometimes avoid holding them accountable just to avoid a meltdown? What is driving your behavior?

5. What research can you do to determine what is driving your students' behaviors? What skills are they missing? What are your expectations for them? How might this influence your decision making?

6. Of the 19 statements posed in the exercise on pages 163–165, which ones did you score highest on (i.e., which had the highest effect on your sense of competency)? How might you respond to that reality? What steps could you take to reduce their effect on your professional work?

7. When you realize you're in a situation where fear is driving your bus, what steps can you take to determine the facts? How can you remind yourself to focus on the facts rather than the fear?

PART V
Live, Laugh, Love

> When you rise in the morning, give thanks for the light, for
> your life, for your strength. Give thanks for your food and
> for the joy of living. If you see no reason to give thanks, the
> fault lies in yourself.
>
> —Tecumseh

. . . .

Life is a marvelous adventure, full of opportunity, joy, and wonder. How I wish everyone shared that perspective! In reality, life is hard, often mean, and always unpredictable. We've got to know ourselves, build strong relationships, and believe in the goodness of ourselves and others to truly enjoy our time on this planet together.

The education world is no different from life itself. Human beings are complicated subjects. Emotions are dynamic influences. Trauma backgrounds yield variable needs and situations. And every day is different, right?

This last part of the book is intended to help you see the positive amid the chaos. My aim is to give you tools to help you manage your own mess. During dark days when you're facing impossible challenges, I'd like you to have access to these three key ideas:

1. **Grace.** In Chapter 14, I share how important it is to show (and receive) grace.

2. **Cookies.** In Chapter 15, I discuss the value of meaningful praise and its role in our ability to define ourselves as worthy and strong.

3. **Self-care.** If there's one overarching theme you've picked up from this book, it should be that you need to take care of yourself. Chapter 16 encourages you to do just that by tackling the self-care challenge.

The great comedian and actress Lucille Ball once said, "One of the things I learned the hard way was that it doesn't pay to get discouraged. Keeping busy and making optimism a way of life can restore your faith in yourself." The busy part is no problem for most of us, but the optimism is up to us! It's up to you.

14

Grace

Make finding the good in others a priority.

—Zig Ziglar

. . . .

The other day, I read a story about a woman who was pulled over by a state trooper for driving too fast. As the trooper approached the woman's vehicle, he could tell she was agitated and emotional. She tearfully explained that she had been delayed in a meeting at work and was racing to the airport to see her son, a Marine, one last time before he was deployed overseas. With this delay, she would certainly miss him. After wrestling with his options, the trooper made a decision. Blaring his siren and flashing his lights, he escorted the woman all the way to the "Departures" gate at the airport, where he was able to witness the emotional farewell between mother and son. Instead of writing her a ticket and holding her accountable for her infraction, he made the decision to show this woman **grace**.

You have probably had experiences of receiving grace. Maybe someone chose to forgive you for something you said or did, to look the other way when you made a fool of yourself, to offer you another chance when you didn't deserve one, or just to tell you that you had toilet paper stuck to your shoe.

Grace can be life-altering. Once, when I was leaving Fresno, California, after three days of training, I got lost on the way to the airport looking for a gas station to refuel my rental car. I ended up in a rather sketchy neighborhood at a gas station with bars over the attendant's window. As I was filling up the tank, a woman walked toward me while a group of young men in a car pulled up in front of me, blocking my path. Then a second car full of young men pulled in behind me, blocking my car from the back. I looked at the attendant behind the window, and he promptly pulled down the window blinds. It was at this moment that I thought I could be in serious trouble. I was still in my business suit and clearly looked out of place. As the young woman walked up to me, all I could think of was to say, "Hi." Then I started frantically babbling about the airport, rental cars, being a mom, and who knows what else. The woman made eye contact with me and then smiled, turned around, and walked away. The drivers of both cars blocking me shook their heads and drove away. I remember yelling, "Thank you!" To this day, I am not sure if she was going to rob me and then changed her mind once we made contact or if she saved me from the men in the cars. All I know is that she showed me grace that day. For that, I am eternally grateful.

Who Needs Grace?

My teenage daughter hears me talk a lot about the need to show grace. As a young woman in high school, she has had to take many deep breaths (see Chapter 5). She is at an age that is fraught with emotional tension and enough drama to last a lifetime! Students navigating this phase don't always say the nicest things to one another, and with the advent of social media, the gossip, rumors, and malicious comments seem to fly around at a greater rate every day. The ease of communication gives the targets of such negativity plenty of opportunities to respond angrily, emotionally, or defensively, or to launch a counter-attack. None of these reactions is productive, as I have taught my daughter. I know the lessons are working, because she has often reminded me to show grace when I lapse into making unflattering comments about someone else. Grace isn't our natural response. We must teach ourselves to access the attributes necessary to show grace: intentionality, patience, tolerance, understanding, empathy, and kindness are a great place to start.

Everyone deserves some grace, and I don't believe we show one another enough of it. I wonder, too, whether showing people grace earlier in life might change how the recipients view other members of the human race. It might even help prevent future harm. I think of the little boy from the movie *Pay It Forward*: as he modeled grace to others, he started a chain of events that led to people making positive choices instead of the harmful ones they may have otherwise made. When we find ways to show our students grace, to model for them a sense of gratitude and acceptance, we empower them to do the same for themselves and others.

Although we can't change the world overnight, we *can* have a positive effect on any individual we encounter. Have you ever read what people write on the walls of bathroom stalls? A while back, I was providing some trauma-sensitive training at a middle school, and I used the restroom while we were on a break. As I sat there, I read some truly hateful things about a young woman and some alleged poor choices she had made. The training was in June, and I wondered how long ago these words had been written there—during the winter, at the beginning of the year, or, worse yet, during the previous year? I thought about all the students who had read these vicious words, and how many times the girl herself must have seen them.

Were the stall scribbles true or made up? Would it make any difference? This young woman was all of 13 or 14 years old, with a whole lifetime ahead of her. How much might this hurtful experience define the choices she made for her future? If this was how she believed others perceived her, how would she have the motivation to do anything differently?

When our break was over, I asked the staff members what they thought this student needed from them. Many knew whom I was talking about, and our discussion about her as one of many examples of students who needed their support served as a catalyst to begin to address this issue in their school. What would it look like if they began to show this student some grace?

Every Thorn Has a Rose

During the training in Fresno, before I narrowly escaped the gas station situation, I experienced one of the most powerful moments of my career. I had been invited to train an incredible assortment of professionals on complex trauma and its impact. The coordinators of the training had brought in about 600 individuals over three days who worked in the education system, early learning, juvenile justice, children's services, foster care, and after-school programs like the Boys and Girls Clubs. There were teachers, substance abuse experts, mental health therapists, and gang prevention officers. Think of any program involving kids, and someone representing that program was likely in the room.

During the training, I asked the participants to think of a parent whom they found particularly challenging to work with, who triggered them for whatever reason. We were on the section of the training that addressed working with parents as partners, and I think everyone thought I was finally going to let them vent about how hard it was to work with some parents.

To their surprise, I asked them to identify this person's greatest strength, and to write it down. You would think I had just asked some of them to swallow a razor blade or eat a piece of moldy cheese. One woman bellowed, "There ain't nothing good about this woman!" At first, some of the other participants laughed. Undeterred, I encouraged her to dig deep and try to think of a strength. She continued to challenge me, and with each statement, her voice became louder and she became more adamant that this parent did not possess a single strength. Finally, with more prodding and some suggestions from the audience, she was able to come up with a strength. What was it? Hesitantly, the participant said, "She has great hair."

This breakthrough moment wholly convinced me of the power of grace and compelled me to make its advocacy a key part of my personal mission. The participant's entire mood shifted, and I could sense that this exercise had been a powerful experience for her. At the end of the training, she approached me as I was putting my things away. She was sobbing. We sat down, and she thanked me for making her come up with a strength for this detested person. She went on to tell me that she was a foster parent and had just received the fourth baby from the same mother. She was angry with this mother for continuing to have babies and harm them with her choices. She was at the point where she truly felt as if she hated this woman. Then she said that she was grateful for the exercise because it reminded her that those babies needed to know that their lives were important and that their mom, while troubled, had value. She said, "They need to know they came from something good," and acknowledged that their mother needed to know the same thing. She wondered how motivated this woman would be to do something different if all she felt was the contempt people had for her and the hate she had for herself.

This amazing foster mom experienced the power of grace, and witnessing her experience forever changed me, too. I am grateful for her courage and her willingness to take the risk of viewing this parent with compassion rather than hatred.

The Unknown Context

We all work with and encounter difficult people in our lives. We may react with strong feelings to their attitudes, behaviors, or choices. The truth is, however, that we don't know the whole story. We don't know why that mother continued to have babies who ended up in foster care. We don't know how her life experiences contributed to her choices. We may believe we know enough to feel justifiably angry with her. But what if we showed a little grace anyway?

Take a moment to think of some of the students or families you know that need some grace. What could you do to show them grace? Do you think you could

- Give them a second (or third, or fourth) chance?
- Engage in some dialogue to determine what their needs are?
- Offer compassion when you know they're hurting (even if you don't know why)?
- Look the other way when they do or say something you find annoying or destructive?
- Listen—just truly listen—to them?
- Give them a break, just this one time?
- Identify their strengths and compliment them?
- Thank them for something helpful they've done, no matter how small?
- Spend a couple extra minutes asking them how they are and offering to help?
- Model grace so that others might follow your lead?

With practice, our perspective can shift from one that asks, "What is wrong with you?" to one that asks, "What has happened to you?" Figure 14.1 shows how this shift from blame to grace can happen in our responses to common, frustrating classroom scenarios.

FIGURE 14.1

Blame Versus Grace in the Classroom

BLAME	GRACE
"You just read that word five seconds ago."	"It can be so frustrating when every time we see a word it feels like the first time. Let's start to keep track of the words that we see often and find some ways to help us remember them."
"You have until the count of 5 to sit down and get to work, or you'll go to the office."	"I am going to count backward from 5, and then . . . • "We are going to find a way to work together to fix this problem." • "I need you all to make a good choice and be where I need you to be." • "I need you to complete the task that was asked of you."
"Nothing I do ever seems to work with this student."	"I am working really hard and doing my best to help this student, but I need more support to find some better solutions."
"This kid just doesn't want to learn."	"Clearly, there are some things going on with this student that are preventing him or her from understanding these concepts."
When a student coming in from recess runs down the hallway or enters the classroom talking too loudly, the teacher • Removes the student from class; • Writes the student's name on the board; or • Moves the student's clip down the behavior chart.	When a student coming in from recess runs down the hallway or enters the classroom talking too loudly, the teacher • Pulls the student aside and redirects him or her to the desired behavior; • Asks the student to go back to the entrance and reenter in the way that is expected; or • Asks the student to take a breath and say what he or she should have done instead.
A student who is frustrated with the assignment rips up his or her paper or the paper of his or her neighbor, swears at the teacher, shoves his or her desk, or says, "I'm so stupid!" The teacher • Engages in a power struggle and redirects the student using a punitive consequence, such as saying, "You need to go and get another piece of paper and do this assignment. If you don't comply with the rules, then you will have to miss recess."	A student who is frustrated with the assignment rips up his or her paper or the paper of his or her neighbor, swears at the teacher, shoves his or her desk, or says, "I'm so stupid!" The teacher focuses on the motive for the student's frustration—perhaps the student feels hungry, angry, anxious, lonely, or tired, or maybe the student feels overwhelmed or incompetent and is triggered to go to his or her downstairs brain. So the teacher • Provides an opportunity for the student to calm down and return to a regulated state before helping the student explore some healthier alternatives to the poor choices he or she made. • Connects with the student through his or her feelings before redirecting him or her to more appropriate responses (i.e., connects with the right before redirecting with the left).

PETE'S PRACTICE

While working at the middle school, I frequently encountered a student—I'll call him "Forrest Fyre"—who had difficulty managing his emotions. He was profane, angry, explosive, irritating, and, at the same time, intelligent and charming. I'm sure you know the type.

One day, Forrest had been assigned lunch detention for disrupting one of his classes. He believed that he had been wrongly accused, so he staunchly refused to attend the detention. I found him in the gym playing basketball, and as I interrupted his game, he flew into a rage. While he yelled and cursed at me, I calmly reminded him that all he had to do was report to his detention, and the matter would be closed. He left the gym, still cursing, and we walked together down the hallway toward the lunch detention room. I finally asked him, "Do you need me to escort you the whole way?" He muttered, "No," so I let him make his way to serve his time.

Some other students and staff members witnessed his display, and they wondered why I hadn't immediately suspended Forrest for his disrespectful, insubordinate actions. I could easily have enforced a multiple-day out-of-school suspension for that tirade. However, I had a simple mission: get the young man to serve his detention as assigned.

At the end of the period, I met Forrest outside the detention room and told him the following story: my family used to have a dog named Carter. He was a great dog, but one day he leapt up onto the kitchen counter and ate my daughter's birthday cake. I yelled (and probably cursed) at the dog, who jumped down and, now scared of me, piddled on the kitchen floor. I found myself yelling even more, until I realized I wasn't angry at him for piddling on the floor; I had just wanted him to get down. So I took a deep breath and led him outside, promising to train him to stay off the counter. At the end of the story, I asked Forrest, "Why do you think I told you that story?"

Forrest looked at me, grinned, and said, "Because I'm not in trouble for piddling on you in the hallway?" I grinned back. "Yes," I told him. "What I did was show you grace. You may not have deserved it, and I may not show it again, but our interaction today was about the detention, not your potty mouth." Forrest and I never had another profanity-laced interaction, and he served all his future detentions as assigned. He may not have agreed, but he complied.

Wrapping It Up

In our professional spheres, we work with many children. Regardless of their trauma history, we must keep the following fact in mind: they are little people (even the high schoolers!) who are still developing into bright and amazing human beings. A great deal of their early life is spent with you, and you have a huge influence on how they develop and who they become. I cannot tell you how many times the folks I have worked with have cited their teachers as the reason they survived their childhood. I have countless stories of people returning to their school to find their teacher, principal, crossing guard, school counselor, bus driver, or cafeteria worker to show off their diploma or to share a picture of their family. How many of you have had students return to find you, who have gone out of their way to contact you to just say thanks or to share with you a proud moment? I would venture to say that most of these visitors received grace from you at some point. The strength in those enduring relationships is testament to the power of grace.

Reflective Questions

1. Think of a time when someone showed you grace, even though you might not have thought you deserved it. What are your reactions to that situation?

2. Think of a time when someone didn't show you grace, even though you really could have used it. What are your reactions to that situation?

3. Consider a time when you showed someone grace, even though that person might not have expected it. How did the situation unfold?

4. Consider a time when you opted not to show someone grace, even though that person really could have used a break. How did the situation unfold?

5. Do you find it difficult to identify the redeeming qualities in some people? When you have a negative impression of someone, can

you identify his or her strengths? Try it with someone who is a particular thorn in your side. What do you discover?

6.   How might "paying it forward" inspire others to interact with more compassion, kindness, and empathy? What might you do to start such a movement?

7.   The next time you're presented with an opportunity to give someone a break, take it. Record your thoughts and feelings in a journal. Repeat this a million times and see how it affects you.

15

The Cookie Jar: The Art of Giving Praise (and Self-Praise)

People have got to learn: if they don't have cookies in the cookie jar, they can't eat cookies.

—Suze Orman

. . . .

Have you ever heard of someone who has been killed with kindness? Despite the old expression, it's never actually happened. On the contrary, we all have a strong innate need to be recognized and valued, and we often look to others to fulfill that need. We rely on external feedback to confirm that we did something well, that we're worthy of love, that our appearance is up to par, or that something we've done is valued. In short, we use external feedback to help determine our sense of self-worth. How many times have you found yourself waiting to receive validation for some aspect of your life, even if you already knew it measured up?

Students who have experienced trauma have a significantly compromised capacity to **self-acknowledge**—that is, to recognize and validate themselves, their feelings, or their efforts. This is a result of their allocating resources toward managing their trauma-induced stress instead of toward healthy development. Kids growing up with extreme stress often learn early on to "cue off their environment" to determine what they can and cannot get. Because they rely on external cues to determine who they are and how they feel, their sense of self is heavily influenced by the reactions of those around them. The more they are forced to cue off others, the less they learn to cue off themselves, moving them further away from their own inner selves and needs.

This isn't to say that cueing off one's environment is necessarily damaging or that receiving praise from others is unimportant. Compliments feel good, and we all require some amount of praise in our lives. It's validating to have someone pay us a compliment, acknowledge a strength, or notice a job well done. Children, in particular, require praise from their caregiving adults, as it helps them develop attachment, relationship, self-esteem, and positive social manners. I like to refer to those tokens of kindness as "cookies." You may have fond memories of baking cookies with a loved one and getting to lick the bowl or take the first warm bite of a cookie fresh out of the oven. I associate cookies with warmth and love. I share this concept with my clients, and they, in turn, come in and talk about the cookies they received from others as well as the cookies they gave to themselves.

The Power of Praise

Every time I go to the grocery store, I get a kick out of the cashier handing me my receipt and saying, "Have a great evening, Ms. Souers." Just the fact that she's willing to try to say my name makes me feel special. Pete talks about watching *Mr. Rogers' Neighborhood* on TV as a kid and feeling all warm inside when Mr. Rogers said, "I like you just the way you are."

There has been quite a bit of research about the role of praise in parenting, coaching, and teaching our youth. Dr. Crone and her team (van Duijvenvoorde, Zanolie, Rombouts, Raijmakers, & Crone, 2008) at Leiden University in the Netherlands have studied the brain's response to positive and negative feedback and concluded that younger children (8- and 9-year-olds) respond much more favorably to praise and, in fact, do not access certain regions of their brains after receiving negative feedback.

Of course, not all praise is created equal. Carol Dweck (2007), a Stanford University psychologist, refined the guidelines for praise in her landmark book *Mindset*. She asserts that praising effort, encouraging resilience, and supporting the belief that intelligence is not fixed will do more for children (and adults) than will simply complimenting characteristics that they cannot control. This has proven to be a handy reminder when my son spills his milk. I guide his thinking away from "I'm clumsy" and toward "I can clean this up and pour a new glass." It's empowering.

Over the last week or so, what is the nicest or most empowering thing someone has said to or done for you? What was going on when you got this "cookie"? What emotions did you feel? How did you respond? What effect did this have on your life or your relationship with the compliment giver?

 Describe a cookie you've received recently, including some notes about the context:

Some cookies seem to last forever. Think of the most meaningful, lasting compliment you've ever received. What made it so powerful? What was the situation that prompted it? Was there something special about the person who delivered it? How have you accessed this special feeling over the years? Do you recall this cookie in times of need? Does it empower you?

 Describe the most meaningful, lasting cookie you've ever received:

Early in my career, I started a file to store my cookies in. I often get thank-you notes from people who have attended my trainings or from clients I have worked with in counseling. These handwritten letters hold great meaning for me and help to validate my life's work. In the dark times when I question my worth, this file reassures me that my work, my mission, and my life are indeed meaningful. For those of you who, like me, are prone to self-doubt, these messages can be especially comforting.

Now take a moment and think of a time when you positively affected a student's life by sharing some sincere praise or a compliment. What prompted your action? How did the young person react? What was the immediate effect? The long-term effect? How did your relationship with this student change or grow as a result?

 Describe a cookie you gave to a student that had a powerful effect on the student's life:

PETE'S PRACTICE

One day, I was sitting in my office when a teacher, Ethel, knocked on the door. She asked if she could bring in a student to talk with me, and of course I agreed. Ethel entered the office with Priscilla, an 8th grader with an extensive trauma history and a litany of poor choices behind her that had us worried for her future. Ethel had embraced Priscilla and served as her mentor.

Turning to Priscilla, Ethel said, "Well, you tell him." After an awkward silence—Was a confession for some misdemeanor forthcoming? I wondered—Priscilla produced an essay she had written for her U.S. History class and read it aloud. As far as I knew, this was the first essay she had ever written. It was certainly the first time she had seen a major project through to completion, and I could tell she felt nervous and excited at the same time.

After Priscilla answered a few questions about the efforts she had made to research, draft, and finalize the paper, I asked her how she felt. She said, "Good, I guess." Ethel hugged her, and they both smiled. As they headed toward the office door, Priscilla suddenly stopped. "My chest," she said. "I have a weird feeling." Ethel asked, "How does it feel?" "Warm," Priscilla replied. I went to the whiteboard and grabbed a marker. "I can diagnose you," I told her as I wrote down one word: *pride*. She'd never felt it before. That may have been the first cookie she ever gave herself!

Our Need to Praise Isn't Always Their Need to Receive

Have you ever had a time when you gave a compliment to a student or family member and the intent of your message backfired on you? Perhaps you thought offering some praise would strengthen your relationship, but the message was received in a different spirit than it was intended. The response of the recipient likely surprised you.

Describe a time when you unwittingly delivered a rotten cookie:

It happens. The key to keep in mind is that our need to praise isn't always their need to receive. Our job is to cue off the students and families we work with and determine what their needs are. When we do this properly, our actions and decisions are based on what they show or tell us. However, in our zeal to build our students up and support their self-esteem, we sometimes miss the mark. Often, our desire to honor or praise them is just that—*our* desire. This can be a bitter pill to swallow, because we know how important praise is to healthy development, and most of us have developed the habit of acknowledging strength and accomplishment. But for some youngsters, such compliments are overwhelming: being so foreign to anything they have heard before, praise can actually be a trigger. The praise doesn't fit into the construct of their self-image and feels out of place. When this happens, we need to ease our way more gradually into the praise process.

Mrs. Evans, a principal I was consulting with, had had some unpleasant interactions with a 6th grade girl named Kayla. Kayla loved to swear at Mrs. Evans and call her all kinds of names. According to Mrs. Evans, every time she complimented this young woman, trying to establish a positive relationship, it almost inevitably ended up in a "%$#@ you!" fest. So we talked about ways Mrs. Evans could ease her way into the praise process with this young woman, such as using side-to-side talk instead of face-to-face talk, since eye contact made Kayla feel vulnerable, and offering general positives rather than specific praise statements, as the latter appeared to trigger Kayla. Over time, these adaptations seemed to work. Toward the end of the school year, not only did Mrs. Evans believe she had established a relationship with this young woman, but Kayla also apologized for all the hurtful things she had said in the past. Sometimes patience really is required.

Self-Acknowledgment: Giving Ourselves a Cookie

How do we strike that balance between being able to acknowledge ourselves and needing acknowledgment from others? If we become too reliant on others to give us a cookie, then we will never learn to give ourselves that same approval. We have to find a way to accept praise from others while simultaneously self-acknowledging our strengths and gifts. How do we learn to do this on our own, and how can we teach our students to do the same?

First, we must be clear that we understand what the term means. *Self-acknowledgment* refers to the admission that who we are is real, genuine, and valid. As opposed to empty praise or blind exaggeration, *self-acknowledgment* is how you accept and welcome the unique human being who is completely, unabashedly, wonderfully you!

Embedded in this definition is the notion that uniqueness includes being special and possessing strengths, skills, goals, dreams, tendencies, wonders, fears, and myriad individual peculiarities. These are wonderful attributes that we all received at birth! When children are little, we think that their self-acknowledgment is "cute." We reward them for their positive self-talk and ability to see their strengths. However, as we grow older, we seem to shift away from self-praise; we even judge or penalize that tendency. Words like *conceited, egotistical,* and *narcissistic* are used to describe teens or adults who could simply be trying to cultivate a healthy self-image.

Our society tends to discourage us from self-acknowledging. This worries me. We need to be able to rely on ourselves to make certain decisions and to be proud of such decisions. We must be able to give ourselves a cookie. In the immortal words of Dizzy Dean, pitcher for the St. Louis Cardinals in the 1930s, "It ain't braggin' if you really done it." Sometimes you have to pat yourself on the back if there's no one else there to do it.

Take a moment and think about your strengths as a professional. What is it that makes you great at what you do? What unique gifts and talents do you offer to the students and families you work with? Write down those characteristics and values that you appreciate about yourself. Be as specific, comprehensive, and generous as possible. You deserve it!

 Describe what you believe are your greatest strengths as a professional:

Wrapping It Up

It is imperative that we provide opportunities for the students and families we work with to self-acknowledge. Because trauma exposure interrupts young people's ability to define their self-worth, develop healthy self-esteem, and identify their own needs, their ability to self-acknowledge is likewise compromised. How can our students give themselves cookies if they're unaware of how deserving they are? We can teach our youngsters this skill by identifying their strengths, their goals, and the work they need to do to meet those goals. We can name and celebrate students' emotions, efforts, and accomplishments. Introduce the notion of self-acknowledgment to your students, and incorporate regular practices that encourage them to give themselves a cookie. It won't require much work, but the payoff could be extraordinary.

Reflective Questions

1. What kinds of cookies do you like? Where do you get them? Who shares them with you? How can you make sure you have access to them at all times?

2. Do you know any students who cue off their environment so much that they ignore their own needs? How can you help them learn to balance external acknowledgment with self-acknowledgment?

3. What do you believe about praise? What kinds of positive comments have the greatest effect on a person? Do context and the individual praising you affect your answer?

4. We can never know which comments we make will stick with someone forever. An offhand remark may have a lasting effect on a child. How might this perspective alter the way you interact with your students on a daily basis? Is this something you can be cognizant of?

5. How can you tell if someone will be receptive to praise?

6. What are some ways you can have a "cookie jar" accessible for yourself and your students? How might you use such a tool? (For example, you could have students fill out cookie cutouts for one another, or incorporate opportunities in staff meetings for teachers to recognize colleagues' efforts.)

7. The practices suggested in this chapter are replicable in a classroom setting. How might you schedule regular opportunities for students to celebrate and acknowledge themselves and one another?

16

The Self-Care Challenge

It is health that is real wealth, and not pieces of gold and silver.

—Mahatma Gandhi

. . . .

Long has our field been famous for talking the talk but not walking the walk. That dreaded term *self-care* has come to mean anything from embarking on an exercise program to leaving school by 4:30 instead of 6:30. We all know the importance of taking care of ourselves, yet many of us struggle with finding a way to actually do so.

Is it because we're so focused on helping others develop healthy habits that we ignore our own needs? As caregivers, we are attuned to our charges' struggles and can often identify a course of action that will help, so we advise them, train them, and support them in their efforts—all the while postponing our own goals for another day. How many times have you started a new initiative to lose weight, pick up a fulfilling hobby, or achieve a healthier work-life balance, only to revert to old patterns and rhythms? Eventually, this cycle results in lower self-confidence, greater frustration, and an even more pressing need to take action before it's too late.

Women are especially challenged with this, as we feel pressure to live up to the ongoing, somewhat sexist expectation to "do it all"—work, kids, housekeeping, cooking, shopping, laundry… the list goes on and on. In addition, many of us believe that doing something for ourselves would be selfish. I cannot tell you the number of times I hear the women in my life say, "I want to take an exercise class, but I'm away from the kids too much as it is," or "I would love to meet my friends for drinks, but I have too much to do at home." Then I hear, "When the kids get older/when work settles down/when summer comes, that's when I can finally see friends more/take that fun class/start an exercise regimen." Does this sound familiar to you?

Comfort Isn't the Goal

It's time to take ourselves off the shelf. How can we expect the students and families we work with to be healthy if we can't commit to our own wellness? It's true that genuine, sustained self-care is an art. And, let's face it: change is hard. Do you feel like you live in a hamster wheel sometimes, spinning nonstop but never getting anywhere? When you're stuck in a rut, you can't keep doing the same thing and hoping for a different outcome. Setting a goal to grow or improve is admirable, but the way many of us go about achieving that goal is severely lacking. We need to find an effective way to get ourselves healthy—and that likely means giving up comfort as a goal.

Doing what's comfortable doesn't always equate to healthy habits. I was working with a mom whose upbringing had abounded with trauma and who had experienced unimaginable things in her young life. She had had babies young and was chronically at risk for Child Protective Services taking them away. She chose abusive men as her children's fathers, and she found herself repeating the same abusive patterns that she herself had experienced as a child. In short, she did what she knew—what was comfortable to her. When she came to me for help, she was terrified. She wanted so desperately to stop the cycle of abuse and to be a good mother to her children, yet she had no clue *how* to do this.

We started small with the simple strategy of "If it feels comfortable, don't do it. And if it feels foreign or weird, give it a try." We began to identify what kind of family she wished she'd had in her own childhood, and we brainstormed what that could look like for her own children. She practiced reading children's books to me to make sure she could read them correctly and capture the content ahead of time. We practiced exploring what eating at a table could look like and what a healthy conversation entailed. We identified triggers that were most apt to get her into her downstairs brain and problem-solved healthy options for managing them. Last, we focused on *her*—what she needed to be healthy, to see herself as strong and not as broken, and to build the confidence to believe in herself.

Eventually, she dumped the abusive boyfriend, got a job, and moved into her own place. Her kids learned to expect stories and a bedtime routine, and the first purchase she made with her new earnings was a table so that the family could eat together. She committed to "me time," and her kids were eventually able to see that "when Mommy got her me time, she was way nicer!" She faced numerous challenges and had a few setbacks along the way, but she did it. She found and relied on her own resilience. And it all started with small, simple steps.

Avoiding Burnout

Our work in the caregiving fields is tremendously challenging and emotional. Our own self-care is imperative in helping us maintain our focus and avoid **burnout**—that point we reach when we've got nothing left to give, our tank is empty, and we have to exit the profession.

I know this all too well, because in 2003 I experienced a bad case of burnout. I was a clinical director of a nonprofit organization that specialized in serving victims of trauma. I had a phenomenal team, and I was extremely proud of them, yet I was working long hours in a broken and deficit-driven system. This left me weary, unhappy, helpless, hopeless, and defeated. My self-care took a backseat, and I was miserable. I'd hit the wall.

It was so bad that when I was recruited by a software company, I took the job. Now, anyone who knows me knows that technology and I don't mix. I still use a paper calendar, I rely on my 2nd grade son to help me understand the latest apps, and there's a running joke at work about how long it will take me to figure out any updates to the systems. So when I accepted the position, it surprised everyone, even me. Perhaps not surprisingly, it was far from the right job for me, and I lasted only nine months.

When I returned to the human services field, I vowed that I would do things differently. I realized the importance of balance, realistic expectations, and gratitude and grace. In my old job, I had been so lost in the deficit that I failed to see all the awesome that was happening around me.

I spent some time soul searching and seeking counsel from trusted advisors in my life. I took advantage of therapy, started intentionally focusing on the positives, and began taking risks with friends. I shared things that I had never shared, processed things that I had never allowed myself to process, and came to terms with some of my truths and experiences. It was rough, but man: the journey was worth it!

The Self-Care Challenge

As I evolved in my own self-care journey, I vowed to encourage others to do the same. I researched multiple methods, read voraciously, and learned as much as I could about this endeavor, eventually narrowing the list of steps to what I believe are the top four components of self-care. These elements—health, love, competence, and gratitude—are what we need to accomplish with consistency and intentionality.

1. **Health.** We must exercise for 40 minutes at least three times a week. Extensive research supports the biological science of this idea (see John Medina's superb *Brain Rules*). The benefits go beyond supporting physical health: regular vigorous exercise helps us to regulate our bodies and our stress levels, thus nurturing our mental health. So get out there, find a form of exercise that works for you, and make it your new habit. Swim, run, climb rock walls, ride a bike, play racquetball, move your arms while watching your favorite show, dance—whatever it is that gets you moving. Just keep moving.

2. **Love.** That old adage rings true: "Before you can love someone else, you've got to learn to love yourself." In that vein, we've got to give ourselves a cookie at least once a week. You read about this strategy in Chapter 15, and now it's time to make this a regular part of your life. Do whatever you need to make sure you feel happy and rewarded for being the special person you are. Take a bath, read a book, invite a special friend to get coffee, opt to spend time with family instead of cramming a work project. So much of our work involves giving to others and being present in the moment for them, which can be draining. Refill your cup, replenish your spirit, and refresh yourself.

3. **Competence.** If we want to continuously grow and learn, we must make it a priority to challenge ourselves. We all have our comfort zones; learning happens just outside those zones. So take a risk and do something uncomfortable. This might mean confronting someone who hasn't treated you well, saying "No," trying a new recipe, varying your routine, overcoming a fear, or going someplace you've never been before. It can be as simple or as complicated as you'd like it to be. For example, I went to a high-ropes challenge course for my nephew's birthday, which was way out of my comfort zone. Frankly, I was terrified. But I knew I had to demonstrate my willingness to grow for my

nephew and for myself, and when I had completed several of the challenges, I felt an energy I never knew existed. Ultimately, the experience increased my confidence and overall sense of competence. So go for it!

4. **Gratitude.** The thankful heart is the open heart, and since we're in a giving, loving field, we must open our hearts. Every day, write down something you're grateful for, and within 24 hours, demonstrate your gratitude in some way. If you're thankful for a person, a friendship, or a relationship, past or present, you might write a thank-you note or make a phone call. If it's something inanimate, like an experience or a memory, just writing it might suffice. This gratitude could be generated by something that happened that day, such as a teller being kind to you at the bank, or an element of your life, such as your kids' health. The more we acknowledge gratitude and find the silver linings in life, the happier we tend to feel. The two most powerful words in the world are *thank you*.

These four elements became my mantra, and I began to call on professionals I trained and students I taught to take on this challenge. The results were astounding. I've received numerous thank-you notes and e-mails from people detailing how this self-care challenge has helped them feel better about themselves, gain more energy, and feel an overall sense of hope for themselves and others.

PETE'S PRACTICE

You've got to take care of number 1 if you're going to be of any value to numbers 2, 3, and 617. I've seen it firsthand: the teachers who work around the clock to prep lessons, tutor students, restructure their rooms, grade papers, and create elaborate materials are burning the proverbial candle at both ends. Heck, I've been that person, both as a teacher and as an administrator.

When I felt myself heading toward burnout in my second principalship, I heeded Kristin's advice and sought what I needed. My outlet turned out to be physical activity. I discovered triathlons. You'll notice I didn't say I became a triathlete; that's in my future tense. In the meantime, I find solace and time to process the events of my life in the lake, on the trails, or spinning the pedals. When I dedicated a certain amount of time every week to exercise, I found my energy soaring, my patience returning, and my priorities balancing.

In all areas of my life—executive coaching, leadership training, parenting, mentoring, and teaching—I endorse this practice. It's at the heart of the ASCD Whole Child Initiative's first tenet: ensuring that each student enters school *healthy* and learns about and practices a healthy lifestyle. When we grow up, the lessons we learned influence our health, happiness, and success as adults.

Your Self-Care Challenge Planning and Recording Zone

And now, I encourage you to take on this self-care challenge. Set yourself up for success by starting small. If incorporating a self-care strategy every day seems to be too much, then commit to once a week at first. I promise that it really does work!

Consider each of the four focus areas of the self-care challenge—health, love, competence, and gratitude—and spend some time reflecting on how you might incorporate them into your life. For the next four weeks, make your ideas a reality. Use the forms in Figure 16.1 to help you organize your thoughts, create your plans, and keep track of your successes. If you'd like to extend this challenge beyond four weeks, go for it. Your future self will thank you for the investment in your happiness, job fulfillment, health, and relationships.

Finally, I'd like to thank you for the amazing work that you do and for your dedication to helping others. Our world is a better place because of you, and our children are blessed to have you. Stay strong!

FIGURE 16.1
The Self-Care Challenge

	Mon.	Tue.	Wed.	Thu.	Fri.	Sat.	Sun.
Health: Select at least three days this week to exercise for 40 minutes. Check the box after the exercise is complete							
Love: Give yourself a "cookie" this week. In this space or in a separate journal, describe what you did to take care of yourself. What did you do *just for you?*							
Competence: Try something new this week. In this space or in a separate journal, describe how you stepped out of your comfort zone. Record your emotions before, during, and after the experience.							

Gratitude: Journal your gratitude about something or someone each day. In this space or in a separate journal, describe what you're grateful for and how you demonstrated that thankfulness.	Mon.	
	Tue.	
	Wed.	
	Thu.	
	Fri.	
	Sat.	
	Sun.	

Reflective Questions

1. Take the self-care challenge for 28 days. Record your thoughts, feelings, and baseline energy level. Keep track of the activities you engage in and how they make you feel.

2. At the conclusion of the 28 days, record your responses to these questions: how consistently did you engage in the four focus areas of the self-care challenge? How do you feel? Are these activities worth continuing? If so, make a 70-day, 365-day, and 10,000-day commitment to continuing. Let me know how it goes!

References

Albom, M. (2002). *Tuesdays with Morrie: An old man, a young man, and life's greatest lesson* (10th ed.). New York: Broadway Books.

American Psychological Association Zero Tolerance Task Force. (2008, December). Are zero tolerance policies effective in the schools? An evidentiary review and recommendations. *American Psychologist, 63*(9), 852–862.

Blodgett, C. (2012). *How adverse childhood experiences and trauma impact school engagement.* Presentation delivered at Becca Conference, Spokane, Washington.

Breslau, N., Kessler, R. C., & Chilcoat, H. D. (1998). Trauma and posttraumatic stress disorder in the community: The 1996 Detroit Area Survey of Trauma. *Archives of General Psychiatry, 55,* 626–632.

Brown, J. L. (2008). *Educating the whole child: An ASCD action tool.* Alexandria, VA: ASCD.

Burns, J. (2005). *Preliminary report—Grant 790: Alternative Education Program.* Malden, MA: Massachusetts Department of Education.

Centers for Disease Control and Prevention. (2011). Web-based Injury Statistics Query and Reporting System (WISQARS). Atlanta: Author. Retrieved from http://www.cdc.gov/injury/wisqars

Childhelp. (2013). Child abuse statistics and facts. Phoenix, AZ: Author. Retrieved from http://www.childhelp.org/pages/statistics

Children's Defense Fund. (2010). *2008–2009 bi-annual report*. Washington, DC: Author. Available: http://www.childrensdefense.org/library/data/2008-2009-bi-annual-report.pdf

Coleman, J., Campbell, E., Hobson, C., McPartland, J., Mood, A., Weinfeld, F., et al. (1966). *Equality of educational opportunity*. Washington, DC: U.S. Department of Health, Education, and Welfare, Office of Education.

Comer, J. (1995). Lecture given at Education Service Center, Region IV, Houston, TX.

Cook, A., Blaustein, M., Spinazzola, J., & van der Kolk, B. (2003). *Complex trauma in children and adolescents* [White paper]. Los Angeles: National Child Traumatic Stress Network.

Dignity in Schools Campaign. (n.d.). *Fact sheet on school discipline and the push-out problem*. New York: Author. Available: http://www.dignityinschools.org/files/Pushout_Fact_Sheet.pdf

Dweck, C. (2007). *Mindset: The new psychology of success*. New York: Ballantine Books.

Egger, H. L., & Angold, A. (2006). Common emotional and behavioral disorders in preschool children: Presentation, nosology, and epidemiology. *Journal of Child Psychology and Psychiatry, 47*(3–4), 313–337.

Felitti, V. J., Anda, R. F., Nordenberg, D., Williamson, D. F., Spitz, A. M., Edwards, V., et al. (1998). Relationship of childhood abuse and household dysfunction to many of the leading causes of death in adults: The adverse childhood experiences (ACE) study. *American Journal of Preventive Medicine, 14*(4), 245–258.

Frankl, V. (1946). *Man's search for meaning*. Boston: Beacon Press.

Friedman, M. J. (2013). PTSD history and overview. Washington, DC: U.S. Department of Veterans Affairs. Retrieved from http://www.ptsd.va.gov/professional/pages/ptsd-overview.asp

Greene, R. (2008). *Lost at school: Why our kids with behavioral challenges are falling through the cracks and how we can help them*. New York: Scribner.

Hall, P. (2011). *Lead on! Motivational lessons for school leaders*. Larchmont, NY: Eye On Education.

Hattie, J. (2009). *Visible learning: A synthesis of over 800 meta-analyses relating to achievement*. New York: Routledge.

Katz, M. (1997). *Playing a poor hand well: Insights from the lives of those who have overcome childhood risks and adversities*. New York: W. W. Norton & Company.

Kutash, K., Duchnowski, A., & Lynn, N. (2006). *School-based mental health: An empirical guide for decision-makers*. Tampa, FL: University of South

Florida, Louis de la Parte Florida Mental Health Institute, Research and Training Center for Children's Mental Health.

Maraboli, S. (2014). *Life, the truth, and being free* (Anniversary ed.). Port Washington, NY: A Better Today Publishing.

Marvin, R., Cooper, G., Hoffman, K., & Powell, B. (2002). The Circle of Security project: Attachment-based intervention with caregiver–preschool child dyads. *Attachment & Human Development, 4*(1), 107–124.

Mayo Clinic Staff. (n.d.). *Resilience: Build skills to endure hardship.* Mayo Foundation for Medical Education and Research. Retrieved from http://www.mayoclinic.com/health/resilience/MH00078

Medina, J. (2008). *Brain rules: 12 principles for surviving and thriving at work, home, and school.* Seattle: Pear Press.

Milne, A. A. (1928). *The house at Pooh Corner.* London: Methuen & Co. Ltd.

Morrison, T. (1977). *Song of Solomon.* New York: Alfred A. Knopf.

National Survey of Children's Health. (2011/2012). Data query from the Child and Adolescent Health Measurement Initiative, Data Resource Center for Child and Adolescent Health website. Retrieved October 15, 2015 from www.childhealthdata.org

Oehlberg, B. (2002). *Making it better: Activities for children living in a stressful world.* St. Paul, MN: Redleaf Press.

Patty, W., & Johnson, L. (1953). *Personality and adjustment.* New York: McGraw-Hill.

Perry, B., Pollard, R., Blakley, T., Baker, W., & Vigilante, D. (1995). Childhood trauma, the neurobiology of adaptation, and "use-dependent" development of the brain: How "states" become "traits." *Infant Mental Health Journal, 16*(4), 271–291.

Public Agenda. (2004). *Teaching interrupted: Do discipline policies in today's public schools foster the common good?* New York: Author. Available: http://www.publicagenda.org/files/teaching_interrupted.pdf

Rice, K., & Groves, B. (2005). *Hope and healing: A caregiver's guide to helping young children affected by trauma.* Washington, DC: Zero to Three.

Shonkoff, J. P. (2009, May 5). Preventing toxic stress in children. *Project Syndicate.* Retrieved from http://www.project-syndicate.org/commentary/preventing-toxic-stress-in-children

Shonkoff, J. P., & Garner, A. (2012). The lifelong effects of early childhood adversity and toxic stress. *Pediatrics, 129*(1), e232–e246.

Siegel, D. J. (2003). An interpersonal neurobiology of psychotherapy: The developing mind and the resolution of trauma. In M. Solomon & D. J.

Siegel (Eds.), *Healing trauma: Attachment, mind, body, and brain* (pp. 1–56). New York: W. W. Norton & Company.

Skiba, R. J. (2000). *Zero tolerance, zero evidence: An analysis of school disciplinary practice* (Policy Research Report #SRS2). Bloomington, IN: Indiana Education Policy Center. Available: http://www.indiana.edu/~safeschl/ztze.pdf

Tomlinson, C. (2014). *The differentiated classroom: Responding to the needs of all learners* (2nd ed.). Alexandria, VA: ASCD.

Van Duijvenvoorde, A., Zanolie, K., Rombouts, S., Raijmakers, M., & Crone, E. (2008). Evaluating the negative or valuing the positive? Neural mechanisms supporting feedback-based learning across development. *Journal of Neuroscience, 28*(38), 9495–9503.

Appendix: Further Reading

Helping Trauma-Affected Children Learn and Thrive

Brainstorm: The Power and Purpose of the Teenage Brain by Daniel J. Siegel. (2015). New York: Tarcher.

Child Abuse and Culture: Working with Diverse Families by Lisa Aronson Fontes. (2008). New York: Guilford Press.

Children Who See Too Much: Lessons from the Child Witness to Violence Project by Betsy McAlister Groves. (2003). Boston: Beacon Press.

Creative Interventions with Traumatized Children (2nd ed.) by Cathy A. Malchiodi (Ed.). (2014). New York: Guilford Press.

Enhancing Early Attachments: Theory, Research, Intervention, and Policy by Lisa J. Berlin, Yair Ziv, Lisa Amaya-Jackson, and Mark T. Greenberg (Eds.). (2007). New York: Guilford Press.

Handbook of Attachment: Theory, Research, and Clinical Applications (2nd ed.) by Jude Cassidy and Phillip R. Shaver (Eds.). (2010). New York: Guilford Press.

Healing Trauma: Attachment, Mind, Body and Brain by Marion F. Solomon and Daniel J. Siegel (Eds.). (2003). New York: W. W. Norton & Company.

Help for Billy: A Beyond Consequences Approach to Helping Challenging Children in the Classroom by Heather T. Forbes. (2012). Boulder, CO: Beyond Consequences Institute.

Helping Traumatized Children Learn: Supportive School Environments for Children Traumatized by Family Violence by Susan F. Cole, Jessica Greenwald O'Brien, M. Geron Gadd, Joel Ristuccia, D. Luray Wallace, and Michael Gregory. (2005). Boston: Massachusetts Advocates for Children.

Hope and Healing: A Caregiver's Guide to Helping Young Children Affected by Trauma by Kathleen Fitzgerald Rice and Betsy McAlister Groves. (2005). Washington, DC: Zero to Three.

How Schools Can Help Students Recover from Traumatic Experiences: A Tool Kit for Supporting Long-Term Recovery by Lisa H. Jaycox, Lindsey K. Morse, Terri Tanielian, and Bradley D. Stein. (2006). Santa Monica, CA: RAND Corporation.

Innovative Strategies for Unlocking Difficult Children Grades K–6 (2nd ed.) by Robert Bowman, Tom Carr, Kathy Cooper, Ron Miles, and Tommie Toner. (2007). Chapin, SC: YouthLight.

No-Drama Discipline: The Whole-Brain Way to Calm the Chaos and Nurture Your Child's Developing Mind by Daniel J. Siegel and Tina Payne Bryson. (2014). New York: Bantam Books.

Parenting from the Inside Out: How a Deeper Self-Understanding Can Help You Raise Children Who Thrive by Daniel J. Siegel and Mary Hartzell. (2003). New York: Tarcher.

Reaching the Wounded Student by Joe Hendershott. (2009). Larchmont, NY: Eye On Education.

"A Safe School Climate: A Systemic Approach and the School Counselor" by Thomas J. Hernández and Susan R. Seem. (2004). *Professional School Counseling, 7*(4), pp. 256–262.

Treating Trauma and Traumatic Grief in Children and Adolescents by Judith A. Cohen, Anthony P. Mannarino, and Esther Deblinger. (2006). New York: Guilford Press.

Treating Traumatic Stress in Children and Adolescents: How to Foster Resilience through Attachment, Self-Regulation, and Competency by Margaret E. Blaustein and Kristine M. Kinniburgh. (2010). New York: Guilford Press.

Treating Traumatized Children: Risk, Resilience and Recovery by Danny Brom, Ruth Pat-Horenczyk, and Julian D. Ford (Eds.). (2009). New York: Routledge.

The Whole-Brain Child: 12 Revolutionary Strategies to Nurture Your Child's Developing Mind by Daniel J. Siegel and Tina Payne Bryson. (2011). New York: Delacorte Press.

Mindfulness, Breathing, and Self-Care

"4 Breathing Exercises for Kids to Empower, Calm, and Self Regulate" by Liz Bragdon: http://move-with-me.com/self-regulation/4-breathing-exercises-for-kids-to-empower-calm-and-self-regulate

10 Mindful Minutes: Giving Our Children—and Ourselves—the Social and Emotional Skills to Reduce Stress and Anxiety for Healthier, Happy Lives by Goldie Hawn with Wendy Holden. (2012). New York: Perigee Books.

The Art and Science of Mindfulness: Integrating Mindfulness into Psychology and the Helping Professions by Shauna L. Shapiro and Linda E. Carlson. (2009). Washington, DC: American Psychological Association.

"How to Teach Your Child Calm Breathing": http://www.anxietybc.com/sites/default/files/calm_breathing.pdf

"Just Breathe" video by Julie Bayer Salzman and Josh Salzman: https://www.youtube.com/watch?v=RVA2N6tX2cg

Kids' Relaxation YouTube channel: https://www.youtube.com/user/ZemirahJ/videos

Lead On! Motivational Lessons for School Leaders by Pete Hall. (2012). Larchmont, NY: Eye On Education.

Spark: The Revolutionary New Science of Exercise and the Brain by John J. Ratey. (2013). New York: Little, Brown and Company.

"Teaching Diaphragmatic Breathing to Children" by Rebecca Kajander and Erik Peper. (1998). *Biofeedback, 26*(3), 14–17. Available: https://biofeedbackhealth.files.wordpress.com/2011/01/1998-kajander-and-peper.pdf

A Year of Living Mindfully: 52 Quotes and Weekly Mindfulness Practices by Richard Fields (Ed.). (2012). Tucson, AZ: FACES Conferences.

Index

Note: Page numbers followed by an italicized *f* indicate information contained in figures.

About the Authors

 **Kristin Souers** is a licensed mental health counselor in the state of Washington. Kristin has a Master of Arts degree in counseling psychology from Gonzaga University and a Bachelor of Science degree from Santa Clara University. She is an assistant director at Washington State University's Child and Family Research Unit (CAFRU) in the CLEAR Trauma Center. Kristin also serves as an adjunct faculty member for the Master of Counseling Psychology Program at Gonzaga University. Kristin is an expert in understanding the impact of trauma on individuals and families and has provided consultation and training on this topic to education and human services systems for more than 20 years. She can be reached at ksouers@comcast.net.

 **Pete Hall** currently serves as a speaker, an author, and a professional development agent for schools and districts around the globe. A former teacher and veteran school principal, Pete is the author of more than a dozen articles on school leadership and five books, including *Building Teachers' Capacity for Success* (ASCD, 2008), *Teach, Reflect, Learn* (ASCD, 2015), and *The Principal Influence* (ASCD, 2015). In addition to his leadership work, Pete passionately advocates for the establishment of trauma-sensitive learning environments, education that addresses the whole child, and the relentless quest for continuous improvement. He can be reached at petehall@educationhall.com.

Related ASCD Resources

At the time of publication, the following ASCD resources were available (ASCD stock numbers appear in parentheses). For up-to-date information about ASCD resources, go to www.ascd.org. You can search the complete archives of *Educational Leadership* at http://www.ascd.org/el.

ASCD Edge®
Exchange ideas and connect with other educators on the social networking site ASCD Edge at http://ascdedge.ascd.org.

Print Products
Affirmative Classroom Management: How Do I Develop Effective Rules and Consequences in My School? (ASCD Arias) by Richard Curwin (#SF114042)

Better Than Carrots or Sticks: Restorative Practices for Positive Classroom Management by Dominique Smith, Douglas B. Fisher, and Nancy E. Frey (#116005)

Discipline with Dignity, 3rd Edition: New Challenges, New Solutions by Richard L. Curwin, Allen N. Mendler, and Brian D. Mendler (#108036)

Encouragement in the Classroom: How Do I Help Students Stay Positive and Focused? (ASCD Arias) by Joan Young (#SF114049)

Engaging Students with Poverty in Mind: Practical Strategies for Raising Achievement by Eric Jensen (#113001)

Managing Your Classroom with Heart: A Guide for Nurturing Adolescent Learners by Katy Ridnouer (#107013)

Stress-Busting Strategies for Teachers: How Do I Manage the Pressures of Teaching? (ASCD Arias) by M. Nora Mazzone and Barbara J. Miglionico (#SF114071)

DVDs
ASCD Master Class Leadership: School Culture (#613028)

Engaging Students with Poverty in Mind DVD Series by Eric P. Jensen (#614031)

ASCD PD Online® Courses
Classroom Management: Building Effective Relationships, 2nd Edition (#PD11OC104M)

Classroom Management: Managing Challenging Behavior, 2nd Edition (#PD14OC015)

An Introduction to the Whole Child (#PD13OC009M)

![WHOLE CHILD] The Whole Child Initiative helps schools and communities create learning environments that allow students to be healthy, safe, engaged, supported, and challenged. To learn more about other books and resources that relate to the whole child, visit www.wholechildeducation.org.

For more information: send e-mail to member@ascd.org; call 1-800-933-2723 or 703-578-9600, press 2; send a fax to 703-575-5400; or write to Information Services, ASCD, 1703 N. Beauregard St., Alexandria, VA 22311-1714 USA.

WHOLE CHILD
TENETS

The Whole Child

The ASCD Whole Child approach is an effort to transition from a focus on narrowly defined academic achievement to one that promotes the long-term development and success of all children. Through this approach, ASCD supports educators, families, community members, and policymakers as they move from a vision about educating the whole child to sustainable, collaborative actions.

Fostering Resilient Learners relates to **all five** tenets.

For more about the ASCD Whole Child approach, visit www.ascd.org/wholechild.

1 **HEALTHY**
Each student enters school healthy and learns about and practices a healthy lifestyle.

2 **SAFE**
Each student learns in an environment that is physically and emotionally safe for students and adults.

3 **ENGAGED**
Each student is actively engaged in learning and is connected to the school and broader community.

4 **SUPPORTED**
Each student has access to personalized learning and is supported by qualified, caring adults.

5 **CHALLENGED**
Each student is challenged academically and prepared for success in college or further study and for employment and participation in a global environment.